بسم الله الرحمن الرحيم

In the name of Allāh,

Most Gracious, Most Merciful.

Knowledge & Wisdom

Knowledge & Wisdom

al-Fuṣūl al-ʿIlmiyya
wa'l-Uṣūl al-Ḥikamiyya

IMAM ʿABDALLAH
IBN ʿALAWI AL-ḤADDĀD

Translated by
MOSTAFA AL-BADAWI

IHYA
PUBLISHING

Revised Edition April 2017

Printed in the United States of America

ISBN 978-1-939256-02-7 (Softcover)
Library of Congress Control Number 2017936416

Published by
Ihya Publishing
P.O. Box 426
Alburtis, PA-18011
www.ihyapublishing.com

Author	Imām ʿAbdallāh al-Ḥaddād
Translation & Notes	Mostafa al-Badawi
Editing	Shakir Massoud
Cover Design	Abdul Khafid Mastan
Cover Image	Abbas Wiswall
Book design & typography	ARM (www.whitethreadpress.com)

Distributed by
Muslim Publishers Group
www.mpgbooks.com
info@mpgbooks.com

The *ʿĀrifūn* or Knowers by God and scholars concentrate primarily on making their faith and certitude sound and strong, and on purifying their *tawḥīd* from the blemishes of hidden idolatry.

— Imām ʿAbdallāh al-Ḥaddād —

TRANSLITERATION KEY

ء، (أ، إ)	’ (A slight catch in the breath. It is also used to indicate where the *hamza* has been dropped from the beginning of a word.)
ا	a, ā
ب	b
ت	t
ث	th (Should be pronounced as the *th* in *thin* or *thirst.*)
ج	j
ح	ḥ (Tensely breathed *h* sound.)
خ	kh (Pronounced like the *ch* in Scottish *loch* with the mouth hollowed to produce a full sound.)
د	d
ذ	dh (Should be pronounced as the *th* in *this* or *that.*)
ر	r
ز	z
س	s
ش	sh
ص	ṣ (A heavy *s* pronounced far back in the mouth with the mouth hollowed to produce a full sound.)
ض	ḍ (A heavy *d/dh* pronounced far back in the mouth with the mouth hollowed to produce a full sound.)
ط	ṭ (A heavy *t* pronounced far back in the mouth with the mouth hollowed to produce a full sound.)
ظ	ẓ (A heavy *dh* pronounced far back in the mouth with the mouth hollowed to produce a full sound.)
ع	ʿ, ʿa, ʿi, ʿu (Pronounced from the throat.)
غ	gh (Pronounced like a throaty French *r* with the mouth hollowed to produce a full sound.)
ف	f
ق	q (A guttural *q* sound with the mouth hollowed to produce a full sound.)
ك	k
ل	l
م	m
ن	n
و	w, ū, u.
ه	h
ي	y, ī, i

ﷺ *Ṣalla ’Llāhu ʿalayhi wa sallam*—used following the mention of the Messenger Muḥammad, translated as, “May Allāh bless him and give him peace.”

ʿAlayhi ’l-salām—used following the mention of a prophet or messenger of Allāh, translated as, “May the peace of Allāh be upon him.”

Raḍiya ’Llāhu ʿanhu—used following the mention of a Companion of the Messenger ﷺ, translated as, “May Allāh be pleased with him.”

Raḍiya ’Llāhu ʿanhā—used following the mention of a female Companion of the Messenger ﷺ, translated as, “May Allāh be pleased with her.”

Raḥimahu ’Llāh—used following the mention of a scholar or pious individual, translated as, “May Allāh have mercy on him.”

Raḥimahumu ’Llāh—used following the mention of more than one scholar or pious individual, translated as, “May Allāh have mercy on them.”

Contents

Translator's Introduction

Information, then knowledge, then wisdom. These are the three stages through which the human rational faculty may progress.

When organized, information becomes knowledge. Further organization turns knowledge into a science. The word 'science' in the modern world primarily evokes technological prowess, followed by other fields of knowledge such as geography, anthropology, and the rest. Religious knowledge, on the other hand, is no longer regarded as science, since the modern world lives exclusively in the material dimension and rejects the idea of an afterlife. For Muslims, however, a science [*ʿilm*] has always been, before all else, something contributing to human felicity in the life-to-come. This is why Imām al-Ḥaddād defines 'useful knowledge' as '. . .that which increases your knowledge of the Essence of God, His Attributes, Acts, and Favors, makes you aware of His commands and prohibitions, leads you to renounce the things of this world and wish only for the Hereafter, and brings your faults, the defects in your acts, and the plots of your enemy to your notice.'[01] He was also heard to say, 'There is no true science, after the knowledge of the words of God and His Messenger, other than the science of Sufism.' This is not to say that the sciences of this world are worthless, for there are clearly benefits to be derived from them; it is rather to say that since the life-to-come is immeasurably more important than the present life, the knowledge which secures salvation and felicity in it is immeasurably more significant and useful than any science whose purpose is mere immediate physical well-being.

Knowledge used appropriately becomes wisdom. Wisdom as currently

01 Imām ʿAbdallāh al-Ḥaddād, *The Book of Assistance*, The Quilliam Press, London, 1989, p. 26.

conceived by Muslim scholars[01] is the force of penetration and discernment of the mind, the ability to place everything in its precisely appropriate location, in the precisely appropriate manner, at the precisely appropriate time. It is also the ability to put first things first, never to allow the ephemeral to obscure the path to the eternal, nor the contingent to take priority over the essential. Wisdom is thus the highest mode of operation of the human mind and the means by which it is able to transcend its limits and open itself to modes of knowledge that are direct and belong to the spiritual domain. These begin with inspiration, then unveiling, then the unequivocal contemplation of higher realities.

This brief work by Imām al-Ḥaddād lives entirely up to its title. It offers a concentrate of what the author regards as useful knowledge, then adds to it a dimension of depth which elevates it to the degree of wisdom. A suitable modern title for it might have been 'The Book of Definitions and Priorities', as definitions are the basis of knowledge and priorities the fundamentals of wisdom. For the Muslim of today, detached from the wisdom of his forefathers, estranged from his religion, confused by the inverted priorities of the dominant culture, such clarifications are nothing less than essential.

Only one chapter, the twentieth, discusses a question of doctrine, namely the problem of the presence of evil and the interplay of opposites in the universe. The question is addressed in the Imām's usual manner, with much more concern for the practical implications of the matter than for theoretical elaboration. The remainder of the book is concerned with defining the Muslim's stance with regard to inward matters such as acts of worship, scrupulousness in acquiring provision, and the company one should keep. Priorities are set for all these so that the reader may measure his internal and external environments against them and be able to mold them in the most fruitful manner, by understanding what such important matters as faith, certitude, *taqwā*[02], rectitude and excellence are, and how it is possible

01 In more ancient days the word wisdom (*ḥikma*) referred primarily to Divine Wisdom, that is gnosis or the direct spiritual knowledge of God. Moving one degree down the scale, from the spiritual to the rational level, wisdom as the highest mode of operation of the rational faculty is the ability to grasp and apply universal laws or principles. This is synthetic knowledge as opposed to the analytic knowledge dealing with details.

02 *Taqwā* an all-inclusive term which literally means fearing God and guarding oneself against His wrath and punishment, and by extension designating everything that

to perfect them in oneself, and by being aware of the kind of knowledge to be sought, the kind of company to be sought or avoided, which activities to engage in and which not, and how to structure time so as to preserve one's breaths from being squandered in futile pursuits.

Imām al-Ḥaddād is said to have been so suffused with the spirit and knowledge of the Qur'ān and *Sunna*[01] that everything he said or did manifested these to perfection. From the teachings of such a man a whole pattern of behavior emerges that is suffused with Qur'ānic wisdom and thus conducive to spiritual realization. These subjects are discussed with such clarity and precision that they remain extremely valuable guidelines for the beginner, the traveler and the scholar.

The teachings are vividly illustrated with stories and epigrams of the Prophets of old, the four Caliphs, the Companions, the Followers and the great Sufis.

The work was completed on the 20th of January 1718 CE, only two years before the Imām's death. He had started it many years earlier and had dictated about twenty chapters, but then stopped. In the course of a conversation concerning this work the Imām remarked, 'Each chapter can be considered a [complete] work, since the meaning [or message] of each is independent and distinct from the others. Also, these are *wāridāt*[02]—whenever something comes to us we write it down. However, this time [we live in] is not one whose people are worthy of *wāridāt*, which is why they have stopped coming.' It is of note that the Imām clearly states here that his works are not simply products of a 'thinking mind', however great this mind might be, but works of inspiration. The function of the rational faculty here is to receive the spiritual influx of knowledge and express it in a form that renders it easy to understand and retain. The Imām then goes on to complain about his countrymen's lack of interest in his works and in the knowledge, he wishes to disseminate among them. Fully aware of the special gift of clarity and synthesis that gave his writings their undeniable

---

can be considered a good deed, whether it is an obligatory or recommended act, or the avoidance of the forbidden.

01 The term *Sunna* refers to everything that the Prophet ever said, did, or saw someone else say or do and approved of. The two main sources of religious knowledge in general and the Sacred Law in particular are first the Qur'ān and then the *Sunna*.

02 *Wāridāt*: plural of *wārid* which is 'something that is arriving'. In this context, it may refer either to inspired knowledge or to a spiritual state.

impact, it saddened him to see that so many people in his hometown were unaware of their existence. 'Were they to peruse only one of our books and study it thoroughly, it would suffice them.'

The chapter titles are our own. A few lines of poetry were omitted where this omission did not materially affect the text.

MOSTAFĀ AL-BADAWĪ

Prologue

In the Name of God, All-Merciful and Compassionate
There is neither power nor ability save by God, the High, the Immense.

Transcendent are You! We have no knowledge save that which You have taught us; You are the Knowing, the Wise.[1]

May God be praised and thanked! More Merciful is He and Wiser than any other possessed of mercy and wisdom.[01] He is the Best Creator and Provider.[02] His knowledge encompasses all things and of all things He keeps count. **Should He not know what He created, when He is the Subtle, the Aware?**[2] **His is the Sovereignty of the heavens and the earth; He quickens and He gives death, and He is Able to do all things. He is the First and the Last, the Outward and the Inward, and He has knowledge of all things.**[3] **The Alive, the Sustainer; [. . .] His Footstool encompasses the heavens and**

01 This is to say that the mercy and wisdom of God are absolute whereas those of created beings are relative. The mercy that a creature exhibits is but a faint shadow of the Divine Mercy. A *ḥadīth* declares that in God's possession are a hundred mercies, only one was granted to this world while athe remaining ninety-nine are kept in store for the next. [Bukhārī, *Saḥīḥ*, 6469] This one mercy is the origin of every mercy manifested in the world. Similarly, the wisdom of a human being is but a shadow of the Divine Attribute of Wisdom manifesting in relative mode and in proportion to the limitations of that being. In other words, there can be neither mercy nor wisdom in the world save those that God projects into the world as shadows of His Own Attributes.

02 Again, this is a way of saying that God is the only true Creator and Provider. Therefore, when a human being creates a work of art or when a tiger provides for its cubs, they do so solely through the projection into the world, in relative mode and in proportion to the limitations of each being, of the Divine Attributes.

the earth, and it wearies Him not to preserve them; and He is the High, the Immense.[4]

I thank Him for that which He teaches and inspires, that which He causes us to say and understand, and for all His openings and graces. **That which God opens for mankind of mercy none can withhold, and that which He withholds none can release thereafter; and He is the August, the Wise.**[5]

May God's blessings and peace be upon our master and patron Muḥammad whom He sent as a mercy to the worlds,[01] made the Seal of the Prophets and the Master of Messengers, and upon his family, Companions, and those who follow them with excellence until Judgment Day.

To proceed: These are chapters of knowledge we have recorded and foundations of wisdom we have alerted to, such as come to mind in the course of mutual reminding, reflection and meditation, and which scholars, worshippers and travelers on the path often need. We have not arranged them in the pattern common to such books, that is, in a particular sequence according to the relationship between them so that each would complement the preceding ones. The reason being that, as we have mentioned, they come to mind on various occasions during teaching sessions and discussions which touch on numerous subjects, some quite remote from the others. This led to each chapter being almost entirely independent of the others, the exceptions being few. The chapters contain comprehensive principles and summary wisdom. Should a scholar of broad knowledge wish to convert each chapter into a separate book, by analyzing its principle and detailing its summary wisdom, it would be an easy task, as will be clearly perceived by those endowed with knowledge and perspicacity and those possessed of hearts and secrets[02], those to whom God has given wisdom. **And he to**

---

01 This refers to the Divine proclamation in the Qur'ān: **We have sent you but as a mercy to the worlds,** [Qur'ān, 21:07] and also to the Prophet's *ḥadīth*, *I am a mercy offered,* [*Al-ḥākim, Mustadrak,* 100; Bayhaqī, *Shuʿab al-īmān*, 1374] and to his title 'Prophet of Mercy' (*Nabī al-Raḥma*), for the Prophet taught his companions to pray as follows: *O God! I ask You and direct myself to You through Your Prophet Muḥammad, the Prophet of Mercy. O Muḥammad, I address myself to God through you for my request to be granted. O God! Allow him to intercede on my behalf!* [Ibn *Māja, Sunan,* 1385; Tirmidhī, *Sunan,* 3578.]

02 In this context, the 'heart' should be taken to indicate the center of individual consciousness when purified and open to the influence of the 'spirit'. The latter's higher most aspect where it reaches the Divine Presence is referred to as the 'secret'.

whom wisdom is given, he truly has received abundant good; but none remember except men of understanding.[6]

When we began to record these chapters, our intention was not to publish them until they had reached forty in number. However, a long time has elapsed since then, the required number has yet to be reached, and a sincere brother of ours, upon learning of their existence, requested our permission to copy and study them. This made us decide to bring them out, with the benefit to be derived from them in view. *Deeds are valued according to the intention, and each man receives according to what he intended.*[01] At this time the chapters number twenty, others can be added in the future, God the Exalted willing.[02]

It is now time to turn our intention into action. God, it is Whose help we seek, upon Him rests the conveyance [meanings]; ability and strength are only by Him—Blessed and Exalted is He. God suffices us and He is the Best of Custodians. **My success is only by God; on Him do I depend and to Him do I humbly turn.**[7]

01 This refers to the opening *ḥadīth* in the compilation of Imām Bukhārī: *Deeds are but by intention and every man shall have but that which he intended. Thus, he whose migration is to God and His Messenger, his migration is to God and His Messenger; and he whose migration is to something of the world or to marry a woman, his migration is to that which he migrated to.*

02 This is obviously the prologue for the first twenty chapters when they were first circulated and seems to have been retained when, much later, the remaining twenty were added and the book completed.

I

THE ORDER OF PRIORITIES

The *ʿĀrifūn* or Knowers by God[01] and scholars concentrate primarily on making their faith and certitude sound and strong, and on purifying their *tawḥīd*[02] from the blemishes of hidden idolatry. They then turn their attention to perfecting the virtues such as detachment, sincerity, and keeping the breast clear toward Muslims, and to counteracting blameworthy attributes such as greed, ostentation, and vanity. Next, they attend to the soundness of their good outward actions and to guarding themselves against falling into evil works. Lastly, they attend to the good management of their daily

---

01 A *ʿārif bi'l-lāh* is one who knows by God, not by means of his own powers and faculties. He thus knows both God and creation by God. The textual reference for this is the famous *ḥadīth Qudsī* where God declares that when He loves His servant He becomes his eye with which he sees, his ear with which he hears, his hand with which he grasps and so on. [Bukhārī, *Saḥīḥ*, 6502] In Sufi terms he is one who has become extinct in his Lord, so that he sees, hears, feels, and moves by Him. We used to translate *maʿrifa* as gnosis, and *ʿārif* as gnostic, but the history of these terms and their connotations make them rather undesirable, we therefore coined the term 'knower' as equivalent of *ʿārif*, so that *ʿārif bi'l-lāh* will be Knower by God. For *maʿrifa* we use "direct knowledge".

02 *Tawḥīd* literally means unification, which in this context means ascribing unity and uniqueness to God. Thus, when a Muslim says, *Lā ilāha illa'llāh*, he means that he testifies that God is One, Unique, and indivisible. He is the unique necessary existent and only He is absolutely real, the reality of creation being contingent and thus in comparison with the absolute strictly naught. To ascribe any kind of power or ability to secondary causes is hidden idolatry; it does not make a Muslim a disbeliever, but makes his faith incomplete, blemished. Ostentation, which is to perform good deeds to impress others for various motives, is one other important cause of hidden idolatry, for it means that one is acting for oneself and not for God, so that in reality one is worshipping oneself.

lives and the preservation of their soundness by being scrupulous, accepting good counsel, maintaining frugality and remaining content with little. Knowers are happy with the bare necessities and are willing to let others manage their [worldly] affairs for them, provided they are scrupulous and avoid injustice. Learn, then understand!

As for the unaware and the confused, they concentrate their attention mainly on their worldly affairs and their physical pleasures and appetites, such as food, clothes, marriage, amassing wealth, and so on. Then, when a few of them grow a little more aware and far-sighted, they begin to pay attention to the soundness of their outward actions, such as their devotional activities. They may then move on to attending to their inward attributes, and last of all to the strengthening of their faith. This is the reverse of the order of priorities recognized by the people of direct knowledge and realization. Reflect and meditate on this and you will find it clear! And God knows best.

2

KNOWERS BY GOD AND FOOLS

Had all people been equally intent on understanding the intellectual and factual realities of faith, they would have attended wholly and sincerely to their life-to-come. They would have shunned the world and reduced their involvement with it to the strictly necessary, which had it been otherwise would have led to its ruination and the impairment of all its affairs. But the Divine Will, the pre-existing Decree, is that the world should prosper until its appointed time, and only then will God's Will for the world cause it to be ruined and annihilated. Since this is the case, the Profound Wisdom has ordained that most people remain unaware of the realities of things and steer a course away from them. This leads them to build for the world, attend to it, and accumulate its vanities, so that they turn away from the Hereafter and forget about it. A warning about all this comes in the *ḥadīth* that says, *This world is the home of those who are without home and the wealth of those who are without wealth; it is amassed by those without reason.*[01]

Al-Ḥasan al-Baṣrī[02] ﷺ said, 'Were it not for the fools, the world would never have prospered.' Another of our Virtuous Predecessors—may God

---

01 Aḥmad, *Musnad*, 244192. The home of the Muslim is Paradise. This is why he should consider himself a 'stranger or a passer-by' in this world, as says another *ḥadīth*. On the other hand, the disbeliever has no home other than this world, for he has nothing better to look forward to. Again, in the Hereafter the believer will come into his everlasting possessions in Paradise, whereas the disbeliever will lose whatever was in his possession in this world.

02 Al-Ḥasan al-Baṣrī (d. 110 AH). Renowned Follower who lived in Basra and was a great scholar, saint, and *ḥadīth* narrator. He was brought up in the house of the Lady Umm Salama, the Prophet's wife and was a close disciple of Imām ʿAlī, eventually becoming the first link in the major Sufi chain attaching all Sufi orders to Imām ʿAlī.

have mercy on them all—said, 'The son of Adam was created a fool; were it not for that he would never have been contented with only this life.'

Divine Mercy singles out a few servants for perfect awareness and perspicacity regarding the realities of things; they are the ones who realize those truths and in consequence entirely shun the world and concentrate on God and the Hereafter. These are rare individuals, few in every time and place. Meditate on this fact as it deserves, for it is precious, and underneath it are matters more precious still! And God knows best.

3

GOOD TIMES AND EVIL TIMES

In every epoch, there has always existed both good and evil, virtuous people and villains, people who do good and others who corrupt. When at a given time virtue, goodness, loyalty and righteous behavior are manifest and predominate, and corruption, error, and their people are subdued and inconspicuous, that time is said to be good and righteous. Such were the times of the Prophet—may God's blessings and peace be upon him and his family—and of his Rightly-Guided Successors. When the time and its people are predominantly evil and corrupt, when good is scarce and the virtuous few and hidden, such times are attributed to evil and temptations and said to be evil and wicked, times of temptations and afflictions.

Thus, are times described according to their predominant attributes, for no times are ever entirely without good or evil. Our current times and those immediately before them are predominantly corrupt, evil and villainous. Good and virtue are rare, and superior and virtuous people few, inconspicuous, subdued and vanquished.

God it is whose help we seek; He is Sufficient for us and He is the Best of Custodians.

4

PRIDE AND HEEDLESSNESS

Proud and heedless people are diverted away from the signs of God, from understanding His secrets and from seeing His lights. He ﷻ says **I shall turn away from My signs those who are wrongfully proud on the earth; when they see each sign they believe it not, and when they see the way of righteousness they choose it not for their way; but when they see the way of error they choose it for their way. That is because they deny Our signs and are of them heedless.**[8] Thus does God the Exalted depict them as proud and possessors of blameworthy attributes, the last to be mentioned being heedlessness of His signs, from which He diverts them because of their pride and unawareness. This is because these are ailments of the heart that, until it is cured of them and freed of their deleterious effects, disqualify it and render it unfit to understand God's signs. How can a proud man understand God's signs when he is conceited and arrogant, and does not humble himself before the truth and its people? God places a seal on his heart, as He says—and August is the Speaker—**Thus does God set a seal upon every proud arrogant heart.**[9]

As for the heedless one, his distraction diverts his heart away from understanding the signs of his Lord, so that he turns and moves away from God. This is why God commanded His Prophet to turn away from such people, saying—Transcendent and Exalted is He—**Turn away from him who flees from Our Remembrance and desires but the life of the world;**[10] and He said—Exalted is He—**And obey not him whose heart We have made heedless of Our remembrance.**[11]

So be on close guard against pride, for it is the ailment that afflicted *Iblīs* and prevented him from obeying God the Exalted's command to prostrate himself before Adam—may peace be upon him. He balked and was too proud, and thus deserving—for his arrogance and rebellion—of degradation, cursing, expulsion from God's mercy, and perpetual everlasting wretchedness. We ask God the Exalted to save us from all afflictions! Be also on close guard against forgetting God the Exalted, His remembrance, and the Hereafter. For heedlessness is a major cause of ruin; it brings on all kinds of evils and afflictions in both this world and the Next. God the Exalted says, **Indeed those who expect not to meet Us, are content with the life of the world and feel secure therein, and those who are neglectful of Our Signs, their home will be the Fire because of what they earned.**[01] And He ﷻ says **They know only some appearance of the life of the world and are heedless of the Hereafter.**[02] See how He first negates their possession of knowledge, then ascribes outward worldly knowledge to them, and concludes with depicting them as heedless of the Hereafter. So, understand and reflect! God grants success, there is no Lord but Him.

---

01 Qur'ān, 10:7,8. God attributes three things to the heedless: First, they do not believe in a life-to-come. Second, they smugly enjoy the pleasures of the world as if they were going to live forever, are fully satisfied with these pleasures, and have no spiritual ambitions. Third, when God's Revelation is brought to their notice, they shrug it off.

02 Qur'ān, 30:7. **They know only some appearance of the life of the world.** That is, they study the outward shell of things, but fail to take into account all the extensions and repercussions at various levels of the invisible domain, yet they believe that they understand the workings of the world. **And are heedless of the Hereafter**: since they do not acknowledge it at all and are thus incapable of knowing the consequences, in the life-to-come, of both their actions and the phenomena they are studying. Such purely external knowledge is illusory and leads inevitably to an initial flourish followed by self-destruction. This is why a *ḥadīth* states that, *God—Exalted is He—loathes those who have expert knowledge of this world, but are ignorant of the Next.* [Bayhaqī, *al-Sunan al-Kubrā*, 20804; Suyūṭī, *al-Jāmiʿ al-Ṣaghīr*, 2769]

5

WATCHING OTHERS

These days, no man of reason and *taqwā* should be overly concerned with the opinions of others and their expectations when this may result in his abandoning things which are good for his heart or in which he can find some joy and comfort. Watching others and being wary of them has become a tiresome endeavor devoid of benefit, for people are preoccupied with themselves, deeply committed both inwardly and outwardly to their worldly affairs, and generally incapable of discernment, which thing becomes obvious to anyone who gives the matter the least amount of thought. Being constantly conscious and wary of others is something that people of resolution and determination have always disapproved of. How good is the saying of the poet;

He who watches others dies of grief
While all pleasures belong to the bold

Watching others may have had some benefits in the past when people were more discerning and had the time to ponder and reflect on what others did. Total commitment to worldly affairs and loss of discernment have since caused such people to dwindle and largely disappear. A person of *taqwā* and reason should therefore strive only for the good pleasure of his Lord, his own salvation, success in the Hereafter, and whatever brings tranquility to his heart and joy to his mind, as long as it is free of sinful or base behavior. In doing so he should pay no attention whatsoever to others, since they are preoccupied only with themselves. Let him attend to himself and that which is of importance and benefit to him in this world and the Next. Reflect on this and be guided—and may God take over your guidance!

6

THE FOUR KINDS OF PEOPLE

The people of this world are of four kinds. On these people's virtue and uprightness depends the world's proper functioning.

The first is the upright worshipper, the divested enunciate who possesses perfect direct knowledge (*maʿrifa*) of God the Exalted and a profound, penetrating view of religion.

The second is the scholar of religious sciences who is well versed in the knowledge of the Book and *Sunna*, practices what he knows and teaches it to others, is of good counsel, enjoins good and forbids evil, does not compromise in matters of religion and fears no blame.

The third is the just and equitable ruler whose outward conduct as well as his inner self are good, and whose policies are upright.

The fourth is the virtuous man of wealth, whose fortune is large, licit, and spent in good ways. He uses his wealth to comfort the weak and the destitute and fulfil the needs of the needy. He accumulates wealth and keeps it only for this purpose, for the goodness and nobility of such and similar endeavors.

In opposition to each of these four are others who resemble them outwardly but differ in meaning and in reality.

Opposed to the upright man of worship is the confused deceitful Sufi. Opposed to the scholar who practices what he knows is the depraved compromising scholar. Opposed to the just ruler is the tyrant of iniquitous conduct, whose policies and management are defective. And opposed to the wealthy man of virtue is the unjust rich man who accumulates wealth illicitly, withholding it when it should be spent and spending it when it should not be spent. These four are the cause of the world's corruption and instability, of the confusion in people's affairs and their abandoning the right ways.

The matter is entirely God's; in His Hand is the dominion of all things. Transcendent is the One, the Invincible, the King, the Bestower. He provides the means for that which He wills, in the manner He wills. There is no god but He and to Him is the Final Return.

7

PEOPLE AND THE WORLD: THE THREE CATEGORIES

Know that God—Exalted is He—to Whom all praise belongs, created the world for the believer as a means to an end: namely provision for the Hereafter and obedience to his Lord. For the depraved, on the other hand, the world is a place to seek pleasures and satisfy appetites, heedless of one's Lord and forgetful of the Hereafter. God the Exalted has filled the world with every kind of thing that created beings may need and the various things that are pleasurable to them; creating them in quantities exceeding their needs many times over. He then permitted His servants to take from the world as much as they need to help them on their way to the Hereafter, warning them not to exceed the limits of their needs, and encouraging them to forsake, rather than choose the world. People then separated into different categories:

Some prudently and cautiously confine themselves to less than their actual needs. When things which they neither wish for nor do anything to obtain come to them in excess of their needs, they give of them to those who either deserve or ask for them. To this group belong the Prophets and Messengers of God—may the best of blessings and peace be upon them—and the perfect among the *ṣiddīqūn*[01] who are their heirs, the firmly established scholars, and the virtuous servants of God. To this group also belong those enunciates who flee the world altogether. The first mentioned, however, are more perfect and superior, for they neither flee the world nor desire it. They dispose of whatever comes to them according to the good pleasure of God the Exalted and His orders. This is the rule for first group; it is more perfect and superior to all the others.

---

01 *ṣiddīqūn* is the plural of *ṣiddīq* the literal meaning of which is the utterly veracious, the supremely truthful. It is used in the Qur'ān to designate the highest among believers, just beneath the ranks of the Prophets.

The second group takes from the world according to its needs, weighing things well and refraining from interpretations and the pursuit of special permissions.

The third group takes from the world more than it needs. This group further divides into several groups:

Some take more than their need intending to give it away and spend it in charitable ways, albeit at their leisure. Of those some are true to their intentions and upright in their behavior, while others become confused and are in danger.

Some take more than they need and enjoy it while remaining within the limits of the Law. They acknowledge that those who disdain the world are superior to them, and that their own state falls short of those high ranking and noble stations. For such people mercy is to be hoped for.

Of those who take in excess of their needs for the purpose of pleasure, enjoyment and luxury, some go to great lengths and multiply their efforts, but are inattentive and mix licit with illicit things, deceiving themselves about God the Exalted. Some, out of presumptuousness and ignorance of God, may even prefer their own state to that of the enunciates, while others may claim that in their excesses and luxury they do no more than fulfil their needs, or even better, are taking no more than the bare necessities. Still others claim that they acquire worldly things, accumulate, and store them for the purpose of comforting others and spending them in beneficial ways, when in reality they are very far from this. Their deeds and behavior bear witness to the contrary of their claims, as does their Lord, their guardian angels, and the virtuous servants of God who witness their wicked behavior and deeds, ugly choices, claims, and self-deceit *vis-a-vis* their Lord.

We ask God the Exalted for freedom from self-deceit and false pretenses, and from all other afflictions and disgraces; and graciously to lower upon us and all Muslims the shields of His protection.

8

THE POOR: PRAISEWORTHY AND BLAMEWORTHY

As for he who seeks the world to fulfil his needs or more so, but it is not made easy for him to obtain that because his allotted portion is less than sufficient to fulfil his needs, this is the 'poor man'. He is not considered an enunciate. However, if as he strives for his needs he is scrupulous and God-fearing, has patience, and then is content with whatever is apportioned to him, he is said to be a patient poor man, and his poverty is then praiseworthy. There are many Qur'ānic verses and traditions to this effect, among which is his saying—may blessings and peace be upon him—*The poor who are patient are the companions of God the Exalted on Judgment Day.*[01] But if in seeking his needs he loses his scruples and his fear of God, neglects his duties to God the Exalted, becomes impatient and dissatisfied with what God allots him and then becomes anguished, vexed, angry, and envious of those people of this world who are enjoying it, he is said to be a blameworthy poor man. His kind of poverty is probably that which was meant when he said—may blessings and peace be upon him—*Poverty comes close to being disbelief.*[12] And it is also what he—may blessings and peace be upon him—asked God for protection against. On those rare occasions when scholars spoke disparagingly of poverty, it was no doubt to the latter kind that they referred, but God and His Messenger know best.

---

01 References for this *ḥadīth* proved difficult to find, however the traditionalist *al-Ḥāfiẓ* al-ʿIrāqī while researching the references for the *ḥadīths* quoted by Imam Ghazālī in the *Iḥyā* stated on p. 1552 that it had been transmitted on the authority of ʿAbd-allāh ibn ʿUmar by the following: Daraquṭnī in *Gharāib Mālik*; Abū Bakr ibn Lāl in *Makārim al-Akhlāq*; Ibn ʿAdī in *al-Kāmil*; and ibn Ḥibbān in *al-Ḍuʿafā*.

9

NO QUIETUDE IN THIS WORLD

There can be no quietude at all in this world for any believer endowed with reason. Whenever he does find such quietude, it will invariably be accompanied by forgetfulness of his Lord and his appointed time. A fool, however, may find quietude in the world for, being a fool, he is oblivious of his problems and what accompanies quietude in the way of disturbing and befuddling things, whether actual or potential. Because of that it is said that no quietude exists in the world and that man seeks in the world that which was never part of it. This refers to total untroubled quietude for people with perspicacity and intelligence, which thing is evident. As for the fool and the mindless, they may find relaxation. This is why it was said, 'The mindless are relaxed.' It was to something akin to this that al-Mutanabbī[01] alluded when he said:

Untroubled is the life of he who is ignorant or
Oblivious of what has elapsed and what remains.
And of he who deludes his own soul about reality
And lures it into craving the impossible.

He also said:

Intelligence makes a man see hardship in bliss,
While the ignorant sees nothing in wretchedness but bliss.

And God knows best.

---

01 Abu'al-Ṭayyib al-Mutanabbī (d. 354). One of the greatest ever Arabic poets.

10

TAQWĀ: THE EFFECTS OF ITS PRESENCE OR ABSENCE

Know that different conditions which occur in succession, such as poverty and wealth, health and sickness, eminence and lowliness, obscurity and renown, are all considered good when in the presence of *taqwā* and excellence [*iḥsān*], but ugly and odious in the presence of depravity and wickedness. The explanation of this is as follows: When a man of *taqwā* and good conduct is stricken with poverty, his state with God the Exalted will be one of contentment, acceptance, patience, circumspection, independence of others, and many other noble attributes. What he will be met with from God the Exalted will be His good pleasure, nearness, reinforcement with patience and assistance, and other Divine graces. In his dealings with others, he will keep his situation concealed and appear to be fine. They will praise him in his poverty and say that God the Exalted is taking him along the same route as the best and most loyal of His Friends and Chosen Ones.

That same poverty, when it befalls an ill-behaved and corrupt man, will result in anguish, anger, and desire and envy for what others possess. What he will be met with from God the Exalted is His wrath and aversion, and he will be reinforced with neither patience, nor assistance. Among people he will be despised for his poverty and neediness, and censured for making the wrong choices and not striving to cater for himself so as not to be beholden to others. They will say that God the Exalted has punished him with poverty because of his poor religion and virtue.

A man of *taqwā* and good conduct, to whom God the Exalted gives wealth and affluence, will be thankful and appreciative of His bounty. He will use it in obedience, spend it in good ways and help both those near and far. What he will be met with from God the Exalted is His good pleasure and love, and be reinforced with further affluence and ease. Others will praise him for his good works and pray for him to be increased in affluence and ease.

As for the ill-behaved corrupt man, who has money and affluence, he will be engaged in accumulating and keeping his wealth avariciously to himself, will be lacking all scruples, and exhibiting extreme greed and similar ugly attributes. What he will be met with from God the Exalted is His wrath and aversion. Others will censure him for abstaining from good works and benevolence, and lacking loyalty, justice, generosity, and other such good traits.

A man of *taqwā* and good conduct, when healthy and whole, will be thankful and eager to please God the Exalted and use his health and strength in obeying Him. He will receive His good pleasure and honor. Others will praise him for his good works, determination, and earnestness in obedience. Should sickness and ill health befall him, he will accept, be patient, submit to God's will, find his sufficiency in Him, and refrain from impatience, annoyance and complaining to others. He will be met with from God the Exalted by His good pleasure, solicitude, assistance, and reinforcement with relief, tranquility, and more. Others will praise him and say that God the Exalted allowed this illness to befall him to remit his sins and purify him, increase his good deeds, and raise his rank.

An ill-behaved corrupt man, when healthy and whole, is ungrateful, transgresses, neglects obedience, and is eager to use his strength and energy in rebellious and sinful acts. He will be met with from God by His wrath and expulsion. Others will censure him for overstepping the limits and for his eagerness to attract God's wrath. When he becomes ill or in any other way afflicted, he will be angry, anxious and impatient; he will be annoyed with God's decrees and exhibit other culpable traits. He will be met with from God the Exalted by His aversion and expulsion. As for people, they will criticize him and say that God the Exalted has punished him with illness and afflictions for his rebellion, iniquity, and numerous sins.

It is according to this pattern that you must observe, reflect, and think about such things as honor and abasement, obscurity and renown, distress and affluence, and all other conditions which may alternate in people's lives. You will know that *taqwā* and excellence of behavior render them beautiful, good and straight, whereas corruption and evil conduct render them ugly and degrading, and expose such people to censure from others and wrath and aversion from God.

Meditate on this chapter well, for it includes subtle knowledge and answers to problematic situations. We could have elaborated at length, however, bringing to notice the little that we have is sufficient for he who is intelligent and perceptive.

And God possesses knowledge of all things.

11

ACTING WITH EXCELLENCE

People of realization, direct knowledge, clear vision and certitude give precedence to excellence [*iḥsān*] in the act over the act itself. This is because to them, the formal performance of acts, whether it be the ritual prayer, fasting, recitation, or invocation of God the Exalted, is nothing but unprofitable hardship and toil in the absence of thoroughness and excellence, perfection of the inner dimensions, and what is due to God in the way of reverence, humility, attentiveness, and courtesy that befit that holy and sublime Presence. It is to this that his saying refers—may blessings and peace be upon him—*How many a person in night vigil gains nothing from his vigils but sleeplessness and weariness; and how many a fasting person gains nothing from his fasts but hunger and thirst.*[13] And ʿAlī—may God be pleased with him—said, 'There is no good in a recitation unaccompanied by reflection.' Some of those who perform the outward form of such acts, but without excellence, even though they expend much effort, may fall into sin. This may happen to ostentatious people and to others who are less thorough than they ought to be during their recitations, bowings and prostrations, and do not perfect them as they should. They will thus have performed acts of worship that are null, will bring only lassitude, and be the cause of sin. Therefore, when you act, be thorough, giving every component of your act its due with regard to God the Exalted both in conforming to outward injunctions and inward dimensions in the way of presence with God the Exalted, sincerity, and courtesy before Him. Thus, will a few acts performed with excellence be better and purer in God's sight than a great many performed improperly and without excellence. Know this and act on it! And may God guide you!

The Messenger of God—may blessings and peace be upon him—said,

God the Exalted has decreed excellence for every act. Therefore, when you kill [animals], kill well! And when you slaughter, slaughter well![14] Reflect and understand his words—may blessings and peace be upon him—*God the Exalted has decreed excellence for every act*, and you will know that the command is general and covers everything. Excellence is the essence of things, such that, when deprived of it, they become defective and ugly or merely mediocre and banal.

12

ABSTAINING WITH EXCELLENCE

As it is incumbent upon you to excel in everything that you do for the sake of God in the way of good works, devotions, and benevolence, so is it also incumbent upon you to excel in abstaining, for the sake of God, from evil, forbidden and suspect things, and cravings. Excellence here is to refrain from them out of sincerity, reverence, modesty, fear, apprehension, and awe of God—Transcendent and Exalted is He—and not out of shame, dissimulation or fear of people. You must also add to outward abstention the inward abstention, which is abstaining as much as possible from thinking about, liking, or craving such things. Excellence in abstention also includes avoiding situations where one may lapse, and any bad company that may encourage or drag you into them. Know this! Success is from God—Transcendent is He.

13

SCIENCES: BENEFICIAL, NEUTRAL, AND HARMFUL

There are a great many sciences, and not all of them are beneficial or of importance to everyone. Some may be so for some people but not for others, or at certain times but not at others, or in certain circumstances but not in others. Still others are harmful and unprofitable, or superfluous and of no consequence. Some of this was discussed by the Imām, the Proof of Islam—may God's mercy be on him—in the chapter on knowledge in the *Iḥyā'*.

If such is the case, a man of intelligence and perspicacity must occupy himself only with those sciences that are important and beneficial. Moreover, he must first of all decide which are of importance and benefit to him personally; then, provided he is qualified and has the time, decide about those that are important and of benefit to others. This is because life is short, time precious, death near, the distance to travel great, and in standing before God he must account for everything, however insignificant, difficult and perilous. Observe in everyday life how each reasonable person is preoccupied with what he considers most important and beneficial for him, hardly ever thinking about what preoccupies others. If this is what people do in their daily lives, how can they neglect doing the same for things of the life-to-come? Although a man who gives priority in the world to the affairs of others over his own may be praised for it, this is not so in religious matters, where the opposite is the case.

14

SCIENCES: THE PRIORITIES

If you wish to know which sciences and works are most important and beneficial for you, imagine that you are to die the next day and return to God the Exalted to stand before Him and be asked to account for your knowledge, behavior, and all your affairs and states, subsequently to be taken either to the Garden or the Fire. What you perceive as most important and useful then, is what you must now give priority and attach yourself to, whereas what you perceive as useless, unimportant, or simply of no great necessity, is what you must neither pursue, nor occupy yourself with or engage in. The same goes for daily life; imagine the same thing and what you then perceive as important and necessary, you proceed with, whereas what you perceive as unnecessary and superfluous, you do not proceed with or engage in.

Meditate on this matter and reflect well, for it is of tremendous benefit to those who have discernment and are concerned for their appointed time, their return to God the Exalted, salvation, and success in the Last Abode, which is better and longer lasting.

Success is in the hand of God, to Him belong all graces, and He bestows them upon whom He will; and God's graces are immense.

15

SCIENCES: THE MOST BENEFICIAL

The sciences which are most comprehensive, beneficial, authentic, and clear are those that are nearest and most resemble those frequently and repeatedly explained in the Book of God the Exalted and *Sunna* of His Messenger—may blessings and peace be upon him. These sciences include:

Knowledge of God the Exalted, His Attributes, Names and Acts.

Knowledge of the command of God the Exalted and the qualities and behavior that draw one nearer to Him.

Knowledge of the interdictions of God the Exalted and the qualities and behavior that drive one away from Him.

Knowledge of the Appointed Time, the return to God the Exalted and the terrors and events that occur then; the description of the Garden that is the abode of the joyful, and that of the Fire that is the habitation of the wretched.

These sciences are the foundations of all others, their purpose and very essence. Studying them increases faith and certitude in God, His Messenger and the Last Day, and encourages obedience, devotion, and abstention from all sins and other blameworthy things that attract God's wrath. It also leads to keeping one's hopes short, preparing for death, thoroughly gathering provision for the Appointed Time, yearning to meet God the Exalted, detachment from the world and desire for the life-to-come, and other such like noble qualities and good works similar to those of God's Envoys and His protégés.

Should you review the writings on beneficial sciences of the leading religious authorities you will find none more comprehensive in these matters than the books of the Proof of Islam, Imām al-Ghazālī[01]—may God's

01 Al-Ghazālī, Abū Ḥāmid Muḥammad ibn Muḥammad, (d. 505 AH). Known to later

mercy be upon him—such the *Iḥyā', al-Arbaʿīn al-Aṣl, Minhāj al-'Abidīn, and Bidāyat al-Hidāya.* Everyone who is true and fair, clear-sighted in religious matters, and gives the matter due reflection and consideration, knows this. Only someone who is dull and ignorant denies it, or someone who is prey to literalism and self-deceit, and is heedless of his appointed time.

May God the Exalted inspire us through His Graciousness with guidance and protect us from the evil in ourselves and in our deeds. Ability and strength are only by God.

generations as the 'Proof of Islam', he was the most influential theologian and jurist of the medieval Muslim world. Although better known as the author of the famous *Iḥyā* or *Revival of the Religious Sciences*, a comprehensive encyclopedia of outward and inward wisdom, he has to his credit a vast number of authoritative works on practically every religious science, especially the Principles of Jurisprudence.

16

SCIENCES: HOW TO CHOOSE

Some seekers of the Real, traveling on the way to God, look at the great variety of sciences and works, and the multitude of paths to God the Exalted, and are at a loss to decide which to choose, so they halt, perplexed. Now, if he who is in such a situation is under the caring gaze of a scholarly Shaykh who has direct knowledge and realization, it is incumbent upon him to follow him and accept whatever science, works, state, or way, whether religious or worldly, his Shaykh recommends or specifies to him; this will suffice to fulfil all his needs. If he has no Shaykh, or if his Shaykh does not fulfil the conditions we have just mentioned, then let him know first of all that some sciences and actions are obligatory and incumbent upon all. These are the sciences of *Imān* [faith], which safeguards one's beliefs, and of Islam, such as purification, ritual prayer, fasting, and other similar things. One must know and practice these regardless of one's particular circumstances. When this is done, one may then choose the sciences, works, behavior, and states that he feels are most suited to him, most beneficial to his heart, and nearest to the good pleasure of his Lord. These will be clear to him if his intention, desire, and quest for God the Exalted and His path are sincere. At this stage, there are great variations between different travelers and seekers of the Real. Some things will suit and benefit certain persons, but not others and vice versa. Some sciences will suit some but not others; and the same applies to works. Some seekers, for instance, benefit from isolation, which improves their states, while for others only mixing with people is suitable. Some will benefit only from divesting themselves of means, while others must use them.[01] The same applies to traveling about or staying put, and other contrasting states and situations.

---

01 To divest oneself of means is to refrain from manipulating secondary causes and depending on them, and to rely exclusively on the Creator of causes. This may rarely

A traveler who engages in what he feels is best suited for him and most conducive to the good pleasure and proximity of his Lord should neither deny nor be hostile—simply for not being his own way or condition—to whatever differs from his own circumstances and the path he is traveling, when these are legally acceptable practices the correctness of which is confirmed by the Book of God the Exalted and *Sunna* of His Messenger—may blessings and peace be upon him and his family. For God—Transcendent and Exalted is He—to Whom all praise belongs, creates for each science those who learn and practice it, for each path those who travel it, and for each station and state those who live and manifest them. To each that which suits him best, nothing else; and He—Transcendent is He—accepts nothing else from them. In this lie secrets and wisdom, the explanation of which would be too lengthy and which are difficult to penetrate, save for those who are possessed of inward vision and hearts, see by the Light of God the Exalted, are well-versed in knowledge, and to whom God the Exalted, from His Presence, reveals the mysteries.

When a traveler looks into sciences, works, paths and states other than his own, he must observe: if he finds his heart uncollected and his traveling disturbed, then he must refrain from further delving into them and steer away. If, on the other hand, he finds that he remains collected and undisturbed, then it is harmless for him to delve into such matters.

Let him know that there are many sciences, works, and paths, and that these are in a general way suitable for all people. When it comes down to details, however, particular people may or may not benefit, or may even be harmed by particular sciences, works, or paths. Their likeness is that of a table laden with food, from which each guest chooses what suits and pleases him best, and is in harmony with his constitution, and leaves the rest, which may be suitable or pleasing to others. They may also be likened to the marketplace where there are many different kinds of goods. Each person enters the market looking for what best suits him and fulfils his own particular needs, leaving everything else to the others. It is not for him to deny or be annoyed by the

---

involve giving up working for a livelihood or seeking treatment for an illness in the certainty that God shall fulfil those needs without one having to resort to habitual means. This is a very special state belonging only to those whose spiritual station is that of 'reliance on God' (*tawakkul*) and is neither applicable to anyone else nor to those same persons once they have left this station for another, for they are then seen to make use of secondary causes much in the same way as everyone else.

large number of articles in the market simply because he neither needs nor desires them; for he does not represent the whole of humanity, such that none should desire that which he himself does not. Now that you have grasped the meaning of the examples given by the table and the market and the multiplicity of foods on one and goods in the other, and that they are on offer for each man to take whatever he wishes or feels is best for him, know that in this regard people are divided into four groups:

The first group comprises those who, beholding the multiplicity of foods and goods, simply take what suits them and neither desire nor are bothered by the rest. They are reasonable, superior, far-sighted people.

The second group comprises those who take that which is of benefit to them but detest all other things and think that nobody can possibly desire them. There is stupidity and shortsightedness in this.

The third group comprises those who desire everything they see, whether suitable and of benefit to them or not. They may thus want that which is of no use and no benefit to them, or they may desire one thing some of the time and another some of the time. In this also there is stupidity, idle curiosity, and lack of insight.

The fourth group comprises those who when they see the number of different foods and goods, stop, perplexed, unable to decide what to desire or choose. You see them bewildered and baffled.

Now, these states may occur to any of those who study the different sciences, works, paths, and states. You may see one of them desiring everything, another perplexed and unable to decide what to do, and yet another holding on firmly to something which is of benefit to him but exhibiting distaste, revulsion and antagonism for everything else. In all these last three there is imperfection, lack of insight, and short-sightedness.

So be alert, O seeker, and understand what we have just said, for it is important and of great moment. Some of this issue occurred with my master the Shaykh Abu'l-Ḥasan al-Shādhilī ﵁ at the outset of his wayfaring. He hesitated much between studying the sciences or devoting himself to acts of worship and traveling. He remained thus for a considerable time until he visited a Shaykh who helped him overcome his indecision.[01] The story is very well known. A somewhat similar situation befell the venerable Shaykh

01 The reference is to the trip that Shaykh Abu'l-Ḥasan al-Shādhilī (d. 656 AH) took in search of a spiritual master. He was led by Divine inspiration to the mountain

ʿAbdallāh ibn Asʿad al-Yāfiʿī ﵁[01], who said, "As I was hesitating whether to engage in studies or devote myself totally to worshipping and dedicating myself to God the Exalted, I happened to pick up a book and found in it a piece of paper which did not belong there and which I had never seen before, even though I had often perused that book. On that piece of paper were a few verses beginning with the following,

Turn away from your worries And leave everything to destiny.

You will by now realize that such things tend to occur to people of beginnings and to travelers at the outset of their paths. I once visited the Knower by God, *Sayyid* ʿAbd al-Raḥmān ibn Shaykh ʿAydīd ʿAlawī[02], and he informed me that he had received a letter from the Sufi *Sayyid* ʿAbdallāh ibn Muḥammad ʿAlawī[03] who lives in Madina the Noble. In that letter, he complained that the study of books had become too preoccupying and distracting for him, or something to that effect. *Sayyid* ʿAbd al-Raḥmān then asked me what he should write back to him. I said, 'You know better,' and he said, 'My own opinion is to ask him to abandon the study of books and refrain from too much reading.' It immediately occurred to me that what *Sayyid* ʿAbdallāh ibn Muḥammad had complained about was what had happened to him as he studied the books and saw the multitude of paths and different conditions. This had led him into the kind of perplexity and indecisiveness that we have just been discussing. We had actually met with *Sayyid* ʿAbdallāh when we visited Madina the Noble to visit the Messenger of God—may blessings and peace be upon him and his family. We saw him and sat in his company many times, benefited from it, and found him to be a superior *sayyid* whose state was that of the people of contraction and anonymity. May God allow people to benefit from him, his ancestors, and all other virtuous servants of His.

---

where Shaykh ʿAbd al-Salām ibn Mashīsh, a Ḥasanī *Sharīf*, lived at that time. There he found all his answers.

01 ʿAbdallāh ibn Asʿad al-Yāfiʿī (d. 768 AH). Well-known scholar, Sufi, author, poet, and historian from Northern Yemen.

02 ʿAbd al-Raḥmān ibn Shaykh ʿAydīd Bā-ʿAlawī (date of death unknown). ʿAlawī scholar and saint and one of the numerous spiritual masters from whom Imām al-Ḥaddād benefitted in his younger years.

03 ʿAbdallāh ibn Muḥammad Bā-ʿAlawī (date of death unknown). ʿAlawī scholar and saint who lived in Madina.

17

THE DIVINE ALLOCATION OF ROLES

Know that you often hear the people of Sufism—may God spread their benefit—say that a servant must be content with whatever God the Exalted has allotted him and must not seek to abandon it to follow his personal inclinations or the whims of his soul. The reason behind this is that God's choice for His servant is better and more thorough than the servant's, and His management—Transcendent is He—is gentler and more perfect, because God has more knowledge, wisdom, gentleness and mercy. Confusion, however, may befall certain deluded ignorant and heedless people. They may think that being established by God in their own particular situation is an unconditional and unrestricted state, a general, unqualified rule. We thus hear some of them uttering horrifying things and coming up with baseless arguments that are of no value in proving or justifying anything. Iniquitous and oppressive rulers will argue that God the Exalted has established them in their methods of tyrannizing the people and corrupting the lands. Rich people and sons of this world, confused and disorderly, taking money from whence they should not and spending it where they should not, will produce the same argument and say that God—Transcendent and Exalted is He—has established them in this state. These are tremendous calumnies and manifest error. To clarify: To be able to say that God has established a servant in this or that, the first condition is that this must refer to situations and states which please and satisfy Him. The second condition is that in his particular state the servant must be acting in God's obedience and traveling the path that leads to His good pleasure. The third condition is that he should desire and be eager to rise to those states and stations that are above his own, in the good pleasure of God, whenever there is a way. He must not allow anything to hinder him from achieving this except that he reach the limit of his own capabilities, but never succumb to indolence, procrastination or inclination to follow the soul's wishes for indolence and the gratification of natural appetites. Ponder these words and study them, for they are extremely important; *wa'l-salām.*

18

PRIORITIES IN ACTIONS AND INTENTIONS

A believer eager to pursue the good pleasure of God the Exalted, attain to nearness to Him and honor in His sight, and proximity to Him in His Abode—Transcendent is He—should hear of no religious virtue or otherworldly good without striving to his utmost to obtain and implement it, allowing nothing to impede him in that, unless it be beyond his ability.

There are meritorious acts which any individual is able to perform, such as supererogatory prayers, fasts, recitations of the Qur'ān, invocations of God the Exalted, and similar things. Other acts are possible only for a few exceptional individuals. Other acts still are possible for some believers who, being engaged in other meritorious or benevolent activities, which in their particular cases are more important and must be given priority, are prevented from performing them. So, whenever you hear of a praiseworthy or meritorious activity and find that you cannot do it, either because it is physically impossible for you or because you are engaged in other activities which are more important to you, then you must form an intention to do it the moment it becomes possible or you have the time. This good intention makes you rejoin those who actually do it, for, *The intention of a believer is better than his act,*[15] and one may achieve through intention what one cannot achieve by action. You may hear, for instance, of the merits of *jihād*, when it is effectively beyond your reach; or of the merits of charity and feeding the poor, which you may be unable to do because of your own poverty; or of the merits of establishing justice, truth, and enjoining good and forbidding evil, which may be practically impossible for you because you possess no power and no jurisdiction over such matters. You must have the intention that, were you able to you would perform these as much as possible and to the very best of your ability. Meanwhile, do whatever you can and help the people responsible for those things by whatever means are within your power, even if only by praying for them, loving them for assuming responsibility for these religious duties for the sake of God the Exalted, and exhorting them to be thorough in their work. You may thus gain as much in the way of recompense as they do, for he said—may blessings and peace be upon him—*He who shows the way to an act of goodness is equal to he who does it.*[16] And, *He who exhorts to right-guidance has a reward equal to that of all those who follow him, without this diminishing their rewards in any way.*[17]

Whatever acts of goodness you are able to do, you must do. Should you have to choose between them, then best you choose the better and more perfect one. As for what you are unable to do, you should have a sincere intention to do it as soon as it becomes possible.

Some good things carry no risk, whether at their beginnings or ends, for example acquiring beneficial knowledge, or multiplying supererogatory devotions such as prayers, fasts, and other similar things. These you must strive for and diligently seek in any manner you can. Other good things carry certain risks, and one fears for those who are exposed to them, lest they fall into various kinds of evil and prohibited things. Examples of these are positions of power, positions of wealth, and other similar things. The intelligent and the wise should avoid and never chase these, for if obtained, they may destroy them, as has happened to many who exposed themselves to such things and thereby ruined both their religion and their world, falling into that which brought upon them the wrath of their Lord. As regards the recompense obtained by those granted success while holding power or wealth, it will suffice you to make between yourself and God the Exalted the intention that if ever you might become established in such a position, you would assume it solely for His sake, and behave according to His good pleasure and in a way that brings you nearer to Him. Through these good intentions you will receive as much Divine reward as those who actually hold such positions, while remaining safe from both their risks and their trials. The Prophet ﷺ once said to one of his Companions, *Never seek command, for if you are given it, having sought it, you will be left to cope with it; but if you are given it, having not sought it, you will be assisted with it.*[18] An example is the well-known story of Thaʿlaba, who asked the Messenger of God ﷺ to pray that God give him wealth so that he could give alms and do good. It is to him that God's revelation refers, **Among**

them is one who swore an oath to God that, should He give him of His bounty, he would give alms.[01]

Anything carrying a risk should be avoided, not chased. Be content with safety, for it is one of the two gains.[02] You may hear, for instance, of the recompense that those who patiently endure trials and illnesses receive, and may thus desire it and hope to obtain the merit for such things, only then to be tested and found unable to endure patiently. The Messenger of God—may blessings and peace be upon him and his family—often encouraged and prompted people to pray for wellbeing.[03] It suffices you to have the intention and sincere determination that, should God the Exalted test you, you would be patient and endure in expectation [of God's grace]. Meanwhile, pray for wellbeing and make use of it in obeying God and seeking His good pleasure.

---

01 Qur'ān,9:75. Thaʿlaba was a man who asked the Prophet—may God's blessings and peace be upon him—for a herd of sheep, swearing to give some away in charitable ways. However, once he had obtained his sheep he failed to give any away. Furthermore, when he was visited by the Companion responsible for collecting the *Zakāt* on behalf of the Prophet—may God's blessings and peace be upon him—he refused to hand over his dues, thus proving himself to be a hypocrite who outwardly professes to be a Muslim, while inwardly harboring disbelief. He was thus not considered a Companion. The relevant Qur'ānic passage reads as follows: **Nevertheless, when He gave him bounty he withheld it avariciously and turned away, swerving aside, So as a consequence, He put hypocrisy into his heart, until the day he meets Him, for that he failed God in that he promised Him and he was a liar.** [Qur'ān, 9:76,77]

02 One of the two gains is safety from the difficulties and burden of sin consequent upon accepting a responsibility that may prove to be beyond one's capability. The second gain, which comes from the more dangerous alternative, is the reward for having accepted it and discharged it adequately.

03 Wellbeing [*ʿāfiya*] is an all-inclusive term which means safety from illnesses, accidents and other outward forms of suffering, as well as from temptations, doubts, and other inward hazards. When Imām al-Ḥaddād wrote to his brother al-Ḥāmid defining what he meant by *al-ʿāfiya*, wellbeing, he said, "Physical wellbeing is freedom of the bodies from falling into sins and from sicknesses and ailments. Intelligible wellbeing is freedom of the hearts from doubts and illusions, and from harboring evil toward any Muslim." It is easily observable that when most people pray for wellbeing, they usually have in mind wellbeing in this world and therefore the outward dimension; but when the elite pray for wellbeing, they concentrate primarily on the inward dimension, the major perils in their view being those that cut them off from their Lord.

You are now aware that you must do everything you can in the way of benevolent and generous activities. Combine as many as is possible for you and choose the better and more perfect alternative whenever you are forced to choose. But you must also refrain from exposing yourself to anything carrying a substantial risk, even if good, save that which is forced upon you or with which you are tested. You must also refrain from giving priority to anything save that which is most important and beneficial to your religion, according to the rules that we have explained in previous chapters, for these matters are interrelated and clarify one another. Ponder on this and reflect well. May God assist you and us with permanent success and guide us to the even road, the straightest path, in ease and wellbeing!

19

THE PURSUIT OF WORLDLY PLEASURES

In this world, those who possess the utmost in comfort, enjoy the greatest pleasures, and are most intent on pursuing them, are also the weariest, most fatigued, endangered, worried, stressed and aggrieved of all. Such is the plight of the kings and the rich. On the other hand, those who possess the fewest comforts and pleasures, and are the least desirous of them, are the least wearied, fatigued, endangered, worried and stressed. Such are the poor and the indigent. The reason behind this is that the delights, comforts and passions of the world are in their very essence troubling, disturbing and stressful.[01] Also, those who jostle, compete and envy others for them are quite numerous. This is why it is extremely exhausting, hazardous and aggrieving to pursue, enjoy, protect and multiply these things. The more one takes from the world and its pleasures and the more one pursues and craves for them, the more one's problems, dangers, worries and sorrows multiply. On the other hand, the less one desires and pursues the world's pleasures, the less one's exhaustion, dangers, worries and sorrows become. One can observe how kings and wealthy people are among the most tired, worried, aggrieved and endangered of all people. Some of them hazard their very

---

01 The higher one ascends in the degrees of universal existence the more one finds that order, harmony, peace and beauty prevail. On the other hand, disharmony, conflict, and disorder increase as one goes down, to reach the maximum in the material world. This is why worldly pleasures and comforts, which appeal to the lowest elements in a human being, namely his bestial appetites, can bring only disharmony and restlessness to his heart. By their very nature they engender disorder. They can but arouse in the soul the dispersing and conflicting tendencies that lead to frustration, anger and other negative emotions. It is only when the upward pull of the spirit conquers these elements that peace and beauty reign in the heart, and the lower elements become part of the higher order.

souls and endanger their hearts in pursuing their desires and passions, or in protecting and multiplying them. This is quite evident to any intelligent observer. As for the poor and the indigent, they are the least worried and aggrieved of all, for they demand but little of the pleasures of the world and its passions, either by choice as do the enunciates, or by necessity, as do those people who are weak and do not even entertain such ideas, let alone actively pursue them. Both have fewer worries and fewer sorrows.

Know that those who demand from the world the needs sufficient for only one day are less stressed and worried than those who demand the needs sufficient for a week; those who seek a week's needs are less worried than those who seek a month's; and those who seek a month's needs are less worried than those who seek a year's. Those whose desires are confined to themselves are less stressed and worried than those who desire for themselves and for others. As demands grow, so do troubles, worries and sorrows, as though the pleasures and comforts that a man finds in the world are on one side of the scales, while the hardship, danger and grief they endure are on the other, usually balancing each other. There are individual differences, and one side may outweigh the other a little, but never very much. This is what happens to the two different groups in this world, what they endure in their lifetime. As for the Hereafter, it would take too long to discuss or even simply to enumerate the well-known *ḥadīths* and other sayings describing what those who run after pleasures and appetites in this world will undergo. They will be called to account, and will meet with chastisement, hardship and great terror. On the other hand, the poor and the indigent hope and expect happiness, honor, success, and repose, as is well known from much textual evidence. Therefore, if you desire rest in this world, relinquish your quest for rest in it! A wise man was once asked, 'To whom does the Hereafter belong?' He replied, 'To those who seek it.' Then he was asked, 'And to whom does this world belong?' He replied, 'To those who forsake it.' When Ibrāhīm ibn Adham 🙼 saw a sorrowful Sufi, he said to him, 'Worry not, nor grieve. Were kings to know what tranquility is ours they would fight us for it with their swords.' The cause of his (i.e. Ibrahīm's) abandoning his worldly position and ephemeral kingship is that he once looked out of his palace window at midday and saw a poor man taking refuge in the shade of the palace. The man took out a flat loaf of bread, ate it, drank some water, and then laid down in the shade and went to sleep. Ibrāhīm liked what he saw, envying the man his peace of mind, so he sent someone with orders to fetch him as soon as he woke up. When the man was brought to Ibrāhīm, he said to him, 'You ate your loaf when you were hungry and were sated?' The man said, 'Yes!' He said, 'Then you slept and were rested?' Again the man answered, 'Yes!' So Ibrāhīm said to himself, 'If the soul can be satisfied with as a little of the world as that, what have I to do with the world?' At nightfall, he left the palace and all that it contained and devoted himself entirely to God the Exalted. What became of him is well known.[01]

You now know, from what has just been said, that the comforts of this world, its pleasures and its passions, are wearisome, perilous, alarming, grievous and painful. Their increase always comes with an increase in these accompanying things and greater vulnerability to them. When pleasures, comforts and passions diminish, so too do weariness, peril, worry and grief, and then one is more at ease. This is in addition to the sorry consequences awaiting the pleasure-seekers in the Hereafter; and the honors awaiting those who forsook those pleasures, who left them either by choice, or by force of circumstance. This is clear to anyone who reflects on it impartially.

---

01 Ibrāhīm ibn Adham (d. 161 AH). One of the earliest Sufis to be mentioned by Imām Qushayrī in his *Risāla*, he was Prince of Balkh in Central Asia and renounced his throne in order to live a saintly and ascetic life, eventually becoming known as *Zāhid Khurāsān*, The Renunciate of Khurasan, and reaching the highest degrees of direct knowledge of God.

20

THE PAIRS OF OPPOSITES

Those whose powers of discernment are weak may observe the opposites in this world such as light and darkness, good and evil, righteousness and corruption, benefit and harm, and so on. They may turn this over in their minds and then perhaps imagine that had the world been made exclusively of light, goodness, good functioning, and beneficence, it would have been better and more useful. They may then raise objections to God's creation of the opposite of these and go on to think that there is neither cause nor wisdom behind their existence. This is but ignorance, inability to reason, and unawareness. For God—Transcendent is He—to Whom all praise belongs, is the Wisest of Sovereigns; to Him belongs the absolute knowledge that encompasses all things from all sides, and He is the Ablest of the Able and Most Merciful of the Merciful. It has been related that *God the Exalted said, 'Indeed I am God, there is no God but I; I create good and evil and for each of them I create people. Blessed are those I create for good and through whom I bring it about, and woe to those I create for evil and through whom I bring it about;*[19] *and twice woe, to those who ask why and how.'*[01] Those who say 'Why?', 'How?', and 'If only', when they see things which they are able neither to understand, nor to perceive the wisdom within, are those who dispute and raise objections to God's management [of His creation].

Know that the existence of the world as it is, with its multitude of opposing and contrasting things, is most complete and excellent and could not have been better or more wisely made, considering the reason behind it and what it was created for; so know this! The explanation of this is that the world can be conceived in four different ways: (1) as it is now, that is,

---

01 According to *al-Ḥāfiẓ* al-ʿIrāqī this addition is to be found in Ibn Shāhin, *Sharḥ al-Sunna,* on the authority of the Companion Abū Umāma, with a weak chain of transmission.

containing opposition; (2) made of pure goodness and absolute beneficence; (3) made of evil and harm exclusively; (4) non-existent. There is no conceivable fifth condition. As for non-existence, it is no-thing and has no reality, so neither can it have meaning. As for pure goodness, had the world been that way, many beneficial things and wise arrangements would have been impeded or abolished. The world would have half an existence, and its very purpose would have been impossible to achieve. As for pure evil and harm, it would have obviously eliminated all usefulness or beneficence. You now know, from what has just been stated, that the condition in which the world was created is the best and most perfect. This is akin to the concept discussed by Imām al-Ghazālī in the 'Book of *Tawḥīd*' in the *Ihya*, where he says at the end, 'A better world there could never have been.' This statement is sound, acceptable and there can be no objection to it. But yes, when he went to great lengths in the exposition of this idea—may God the Exalted have mercy on him—verbal expression proved too limited to express the meaning as intended, then a problem arose and a resultant misunderstanding. The intention of the Imām was sound and the meaning he aimed at noble and subtle. Such is, however, the usual pattern when a scholar who is also a Knower seeks to convey subtle meanings to those unable to grasp them. Matters become more obscure and problematic, and the scholar becomes a target for the objections of those who are neither qualified, nor well versed in such knowledge.

Know now that the existence of the world as it contains many signs indicating the Names of God the Exalted and His Attributes, which thing is possible only because the world is as it is. There are also signs referring to Next-worldly matters, which again are only possible with the world being as it is. Moreover, there are signs concerning this world, which are possible only because it is as it is. This is because light can be known only by the presence of its opposite, namely darkness; good can be known only by the presence of evil; and this also applies to virtue and corruption, benefit and harm, health and sickness, and so on.

Be attentive to what we have explained in this chapter, for these are noble meanings and subtle truths that need to be fully explained and clarified by many words and lengthy expositions.

God says the truth and He guides to the way.

21

DIRECT KNOWLEDGE OR HEEDLESSNESS

The noblest, most honorable, eminent, and exceptional people in both this world and the Next are the people of knowledge and direct knowledge of God, and of obedience and *taqwā*. This is entirely clear and indisputable; it is obvious and common knowledge for both the elite and the common people. However, because perseverance in obedience and *taqwā* of God—Transcendent is He—is hard for the soul, runs counter to its passions and disturbs its quest for ephemeral pleasures, most people evade them despite their awareness that obedience and *taqwā* bring dignity, honor, nobility and high rank in both this world and the Next. They are more inclined to follow their passions and pleasures, even the illicit and prohibited, despite their awareness that these attract shame, humiliation and degradation. They thus prefer to submit to the soul's inclinations and obtain immediate—however villainous—gratification.

Know that among God the Exalted's servants, people of direct knowledge and obedience are like the favorites among a king's slaves, those he trusts with his secrets and treasury, who are allowed into his presence, converse with him, are his close servants, and take from this privileged presence the orders they carry out. Who then can be more esteemed and honorable than those who have this privileged position near the king? To God does the Highest Similitude belong. As for people of passions, distraction and sin, they are like the ones among the king's slaves who are in charge of the stables, clean the dirt, and do other such lowly and repulsive jobs. Observe the difference between the two groups and choose the better one for yourself. Know that had not God the Exalted promised the people of direct knowledge, obedience and *taqwā* such honor in the Hereafter, the honor, elevation, dignity and majesty which He grants them in this world, both in His sight and vis-à-vis His servants, would have sufficed them and constituted the greatest of wages and rewards. Nevertheless, He has promised to give them, in His Garden and His Abode of Honor, that which 'no eye has ever seen, no ear ever heard, and no heart ever imagined'. Similarly, had God—Transcendent and Exalted is He—not threatened those who are devoted to their passions and fall into transgressions with being questioned, veiled, punished, and harshly tormented in the Hereafter, the shame, humiliation, and degradation that they suffer in this world should suffice them and constitute the greatest of penalties and punishments.

Reflect on this chapter—may God have mercy on you—and study it well. God it is Who grants success.

22

THE PEOPLE OF THIS WORLD AND THOSE OF THE NEXT

When the people of this world, the distracted and those who mix good with evil acts, give their love to the people of the Hereafter, the practicing scholars, the saints and the virtuous, when they envy their obedience and attentiveness to God—High and Majestic is He!—and revere them for it, they are acting well and in obedience, and it is for them a sign of good fortune and success. It may even attract and lead them to emulate those people of virtue, tread their paths, engage in the good works they do, and acquire their praiseworthy attributes. This does in fact frequently occur. We have heard that a group of heedless and mixed-up people gathered one day and sent one of their number with twenty *dirhams* to buy fruits, perfume and other things to enliven their gathering. He went to the market and found everyone crowding around a watermelon, each eager to buy it, the reason being that Bishr ibn al-Ḥārith[01] had touched it with his hand. The man bought it for all the money he had and took it back to his companions. It had taken him long to return, so they asked him, 'You took such a long time, yet return with only this watermelon?' He replied, 'This watermelon possesses something wondrous!' They asked what that might be, and he said, 'Bishr ibn al-Ḥārith has touched it with his hand and I competed for it until I acquired it for all the money.' They asked, 'And who might this Bishr be?' 'A servant,' he replied, 'who has obeyed God and was honored by Him!' Hearing this they exclaimed to each other: 'If the man of obedience ends up being so honored by God the Exalted in this world, how will it be for him in the Hereafter?' They all repented and abandoned their frivolous and futile activities.

---

01 Bishr ibn al-Ḥārith, better known as Bishr al-Ḥāfī 'The Barefoot' (d. 227 AH). A much-loved saint of Baghdad.

Events like these are frequent occurrences for unaware and heedless people when they take to respecting and loving those possessed of *taqwā* and attentiveness to God.

On the other hand, when people of the Hereafter and of attentiveness give their love to the unaware and mixed-up people of the world, begin to appreciate them, find their condition pleasant, and envy their enjoyment of the world's passions and manifold pleasures, this indicates that their power of discernment is weak, their resolution crumbling, and that they have little or no sincerity in their traveling toward God the Exalted and the Hereafter. Just as this world is vile and insignificant, with all that it contains, so too is he who has desire, greed and attachment for its passions and pleasures, and is excessively concerned with acquiring and developing them. Thus, when people of the Hereafter become such that they envy and respect those of that description, they may end up even lowlier than them in degree, lesser in goodness, and baser in ambition. On the contrary, people of religion and the Hereafter must raise their ambition, rise above finding security in the world and its people, and be repelled and disgusted by all its passions and fleeting pleasures; for in reality these are but foul, defiling filth. The world has been likened to putrid carrion and to disgusting refuse, in the words of the Messenger of God himself—may blessings and peace be upon him and on his family—and those of the Righteous Predecessors: the world is putrid carrion, says one *ḥadīth*[01]. It was likened to that filth which is expelled from man's gut in the ḥadīth of al-Ḍaḥḥāk.[02] Al-Fuḍayl ibn 'Iyāḍ[03] ≉ said, "Were I to be told, 'Take the world; it is licit,

---

01 This was not said by the Prophet—may God's blessings and peace be upon him—but by Imām 'Alī—may God be pleased with him—who said, "The world is but carrion; he who desires it should endure pulling with the dogs."

02 Al-Ḍaḥḥāk ibn Sufyān al-Kilābī (d. 11 AH). Companion of the Prophet—may God's blessings and peace be upon him and his family. He called his tribe of Kilāb to Islam and when they refused fought them, then taught them the laws of Islam and was appointed by the Prophet—may God's blessings and peace be upon him and his family—as *Zakāt* collector. He narrated that the Prophet—may God's blessings and peace be upon him—had said, *God has given as an example of this world what comes out of ma*n. [Aḥmad, *Musnad*, 15747]

03 Al-Fuḍayl ibn 'Iyāḍ (d. 187 AH). Early Sufi and *ḥadīth* scholar who was born in Samarqand, grew up in a village in the vicinity of Merv in Khurasan, then moved to Iraq and started his career by being a highwayman of some renown, terrorizing

there will be no asking to account!' I would still be as repelled by it as any of you is repelled by a carcass he passes by, and which he fears may foul his clothes." Al-Yāfiʿī ﷺ relates in one of his books the story of the vizier who once went out with a magnificent escort which so impressed a group of strangers that they kept enquiring who he was, until a woman by the roadside replied, 'How long will you go on asking, "Who is this? Who is this?" This is a servant who has fallen from the consideration of God the Exalted and has been afflicted by Him with that which you now behold.' Overhearing this, the vizier returned to the king, requesting to be relieved from office. Then, as a penitent, he went to Mecca the Noble, where he remained until he died.

When people of religion and the Hereafter behold worldly people eager to accumulate and preoccupied with passions, they must feel sorry for them and pray that they should be freed and saved from what they have fallen prey to in turning away from God the Exalted and heedlessness of the Hereafter, which is their becoming and their appointed time. God forbid that the people of the Hereafter should wish to become like them! It is only so with those who lack discernment, sincerity with God the Exalted, true detachment, or desire for the better and more permanent Last Abode. He who is so will have exchanged that which is better and longer lasting for that which is base. He will have failed to appreciate the value of God's favor to him when He chose for him to have him press toward Him and the permanent Last Abode, and preserved him from the affliction of turning away and forgetting Him—August and Majestic is He—in the pursuit of this ephemeral, lowly, valueless world. The Messenger of God ﷺ said, *Had the world weighed in the sight of God so much as the wing of a gnat, He would never have given a disbeliever a sip of its water*![20] There are many other well known *ḥadīths* in this regard.

Success is in the hand of God; the whole matter belongs to Him; there is neither ability nor power save by God—Transcendent and Exalted is He.

---

travelers. His conversion to the path of God is reported in Imām Qushayrī's *Risāla*. He became a student of *ḥadīth* and noted Sufi and moved to Mecca where he died.

23

THE GOLDEN MEAN

Know that moderation and steering a middle course are required and recommended in all affairs. It has been handed down that, *The best of things are the middle ones.*[21] *Moderation, deliberation and graceful manners are one of twenty-five parts of Prophethood.*[22] The Commander of the Faithful, ʿAlī—may God honor his countenance—said, 'Keep to the middle course, for those who exceed it return to it and those who fall short of it rejoin it.' It is out of incapacity or neglect that one falls short of the middle course and moderation, while to exceed it is to be immoderate and extravagant. Both are reprehensible and distasteful, in both devotional and ordinary activities, from both rational and legal points of view. God—Blessed and Exalted is He—has shown humanity the way to moderation and the middle way as concerns spending, which is one of the best activities and personal attributes. He said— Exalted is He—**Let not your hand be tied to your neck, nor open it altogether, lest you sit down blamed and regretful.**[23] And He said—Exalted is He—**And those who, when they spend, are neither wasteful nor grudging, but stand firmly between the two.**[24]

All praiseworthy attributes and activities should be judged according to this rule. To go into this in detail would be too lengthy, so we will give only a few examples. Liberality and spending are one instance, about which you have just heard what God the Exalted says. Excess and immoderation here amount to squandering and wastefulness, and God likes not the wasteful; while on the other hand insufficiency and neglect amount to avarice and greed, and the miser is remote from both God the Exalted and from men. Again, courage is a praiseworthy quality and commendable behavior. However, immoderation turns it into recklessness and unnecessary risk-taking, whereas insufficiency turns it into cowardice and disgrace. Humility is also praiseworthy, but when excessive it turns into obsequiousness and humiliation, and, when insufficient, into arrogance and vanity. The same applies to modesty which in itself is exceedingly praiseworthy, yet when excessive it becomes effeminacy and a weakness, and when insufficient boorishness and ineptness. Lastly, good humor and cheerfulness: too much leads to fatuousness and triviality, while too little leads to offensiveness and estrangement. Other traits can be gauged in the same manner. The same principle applies to daily activities such as sleep, food, clothes, and so on; one must always take the middle way, for both extremes are blameworthy.

Now know that the limits of moderation may not be evident, and the middle way difficult to locate, except for those who have religious insight and are well versed in knowledge and certitude. Therefore, any person who experiences problems in this area must refer to such people, and if, as frequently occurs these days, he cannot find any of them, he must halt and wait until he is sure what the right thing to do might be. The best course of action, when confusion occurs, is to lean slightly on the side of excess in praiseworthy things such as humility, liberality, and modesty; and slightly on the side of frugality in habitual things such as eating, sleeping and talking. This only when confusion occurs, for the praiseworthy thing is to keep to the middle way. It is in the nature of the soul to lean toward excess and lack of restraint in habitual things and toward insufficiency and neglect in matters of religion. It is therefore wise and appropriate to go against the soul's inclination on both accounts—God the Exalted willing. The Proof of Islam ﷺ has given similar indications in his writings. To explain further: if a man giving charity is undecided as to whether he is being miserly or prodigal, let him go a little more toward the side of excess, for this is better than avarice. The soul is inclined to like money and to dislike parting from it, so that it must therefore always stand accused of miserliness. If a man is undecided whether he is excessively or insufficiently humble, let him move a little more toward humility, for the same reason. As for habitual things, if, for example, he cannot decide whether he is taking the right amount of food or sleep, let him move toward reduction and economy, for the soul again stands accused here, and any reduction in such things is unreservedly praiseworthy, so long as it does not affect one's mind or body adversely. Understand these things, for they are important!

Then know—may God have mercy on you—that some people of virtue and Sufism have been said to do things which one may think go beyond moderation and the limits of the middle way, being overzealous in their acts of worship, while reducing their habitual things to such an extent as to reach the limits of human endurance. If they are people of beginnings, these things are taken to indicate their resolution to discipline the soul, train it, refine its character and reduce its density. This can be achieved satisfactorily only by means which may resemble immoderation and overstepping the limits, for the soul is like an unruly obstinate animal which can only be tamed and trained for riding and work by reducing its fodder and imposing hard tasks on it. When it loses its willfulness, and becomes compliant, then it is led back to the middle way. This is the explanation of all that is said about such people early in their careers; and these are sound practices, quite compatible with wisdom and correct management. If, on the other hand, they are people of endings,[01] then these things are to be understood as the consequence of being overcome by spiritual states so that their secrets[02] are overwhelmed by lights and unveiling of mysteries. At this point the servant departs from the exigencies of his humanity and becomes in most respects more like the Noble Angels. This state is not perpetual, for it occurs at times and not at others, and should be conceded to those it occurs to. Such states are beyond their control and should be considered norm-breaking *karāmāt*. An example is what has been related about Shaykh Sahl ibn ʿAbdallāh[03] ﷺ who used to eat only once every fifteen days and not at all during *Ramaḍān*. Another is that of Abū ʿUbayd al-Buṣrī[04] ﷺ who, during *Ramaḍān*, entered his house and told his wife to bolt the door and leave a small opening through which she threw him a loaf of bread every night. At the end of the month she unlocked the door only to find thirty loaves stacked in one corner. Others have been said to eat once a year, and our master, the *Quṭb* al-Muqaddam Muḥammad ibn ʿAlī Bā-ʿAlawī[05]—may God have mercy on him and grant people to benefit from him—remained

01 People of beginnings are those who are in their early steps along the path. People of endings are those who have passed through the state of extinction to reach that of subsistence.

02 The term 'secret' here again refers to that higher most aspect of the spirit that receives the Divine Effulgence.

03 Sahl ibn ʿAbdallāh al-Tustarī (d. 283 AH). Famous early Sufi from Tustar in Persia.

04 Abū ʿUbayd al-Buṣrī (d. 245 AH). Famous early Sufi from Syria.

05 Al-Faqīh al-Muqaddam Muḥammad ibn ʿAlī Bā-ʿAlawī (d. 653 AH). Illustrious Bā-ʿAlawī Imām who mastered the sciences of Sacred Law to the extent of being

four months near the end of his life with neither food nor drink. On his last day, they forced some food into him, and when he felt it he opened his eyes and said something like 'have you grown impatient with me?' after which he passed away into the good pleasure of God the Exalted. There are many similar stories about both people of beginnings and people of endings; their explanation is as we have stated above. However, they can be understood in more ways than one, all of which are acceptable and to be conceded to them, may God cause us to benefit from them!

considered an independent jurist and the first to introduce Sufi techniques to Ḥadramawt, thus becoming the spiritual master of all subsequent Bā-ʿAlawīs.

24

GENTLENESS

Know that gentleness is required in all things and is encouraged and approved by both Sacred Law and common sense. Things can be achieved by gentleness that cannot even remotely be achieved by severity and coercion. Gentleness is the attribute of the wise and the compassionate among those servants of God whom He has selected. God the Exalted thus describes His Prophet, the Lord of Mankind—may blessings and peace be upon him—**It was by the mercy of God that you were lenient with them, for had you been stern and coarse of heart they would have dispersed from around you.**[25] And he says—Exalted is He—**Hold to forgiveness, enjoin kindness, and turn away from the ignorant.**[26] And, **And the servants of the All-Merciful are those who walk gently upon earth and when the ignorant address them, say: Peace!**[27]

And the Messenger of God—may blessings and peace be upon him and his family—said, *God is Gentle and loves gentleness in all things.*[28] And he ﷺ said *Gentleness never accompanies anything without embellishing it, and is never taken out of anything without disgracing it.*[29]

Gentleness is to manage things with tact, facility, dignity and deliberation. ʿAisha[01] said that he—may blessings and peace be upon him—was 'never given to choose between two things but that he chose the easier, so long as it was not sinful; but when it was sinful, he was the remotest of people from it.'[30]

Those who most particularly need to use gentleness are those who occupy high positions of either religious or worldly responsibility. With gentleness, they can win people over and adroitly manage their affairs, thus becoming supported by the majority and gaining many followers, so that

---

01 ʿA'isha (d. 58 AH). Daughter of Abū Bakr al-Ṣiddīq and third wife of the Prophet—may God's blessings and peace be upon him and his family. She was an authoritative jurist and prolific narrator of *ḥadīth*.

people are able to benefit from them fully. In contrast, leaders who set aside gentleness and take to harshness and force never enjoy wide support. Even when some appear to have such support, it can be no more than superficial, while inwardly there will be hatred, revulsion and feelings of oppression. Thus, gentleness is entirely good, and no intelligent person should try to accomplish anything without it, especially when dealing with others, first of all one's family and servants, and then everyone else. It should never be overlooked, for it always yields the required results, even if not immediately. On some rare occasions, however, gentleness may be ineffective, especially when dealing with certain mean and ignoble natures. To treat such people with gentleness would be harmful to them; rather, they should be treated in an apparently harsh and severe manner, but with the intention of reforming them and correcting their behavior. A certain Knower by God once said, 'Some people are only shells devoid of reason. If you do not overpower them they will overpower you.' Not far removed from this is al-Mutanabbī's saying:

You win the noble when you honor him,
But with the vile it only breeds insolence.
For graciousness where the sword should be
Is no less pernicious than the reverse.

But these are rare instances, involving deviant people of weak intelligence who have little good in them, being ignorant and foolish, with vicious natures and beastly souls. They are the only ones to be treated harshly, but with the aim of reforming them and as a protection against their viciousness. This explains why, on certain occasions and with certain people, great men of God can be rigorous. Thus, gentleness is the principle and the rule to cleave to except when it is feared that a worker of corruption may thereby step up his corruption and transgressions and it is felt that he can be stopped only by a certain amount of severity and harshness. The Messenger of God ﷺ enjoined gentleness and behaved gently in most situations, as will be well-known to anyone familiar with his history, *ḥadīth*, and pattern in teaching the ignorant and dealing with the near and far. One example of this is the well-known *ḥadīth* of the bedouin who passed water in the mosque.[01] Another example is that of the bedouin who, discontented with

01 A bedouin fresh from the desert once entered the Prophet's mosque in Madina,

a donation from the Prophet—may blessings and peace be upon him and his family—spoke impertinently. When the Muslims made for him, they were stopped by the Prophet ﷺ who instead increased his donation and went on increasing it until he was satisfied and spoke graciously.[01] The third example is that of the young man who said to the Messenger of God—may blessings and peace be upon him—'O Messenger of God! Grant me permission to commit adultery!' He replied—may peace be upon him—*Would you approve of it for your daughter?* He answered, 'No!' So he said, *Similarly, other people do not approve of it for their daughters.* He then passed his hand over the young man's chest and prayed for him, and from then on nothing was more abhorrent to him than adultery.[31] There are many other such stories that have been narrated about him—may God's blessings be upon him—as well as about the leaders after him, the scholars, and the virtuous among our rightly-guided Predecessors and their Successors. So be gentle in all matters—may God have mercy on you—it is a blessing and its consequences are good. **But none are granted it save those who are patient, and none is granted it save one who is immensely fortunate.**[32]

---

walked up to the wall and proceeded to pass water. The Companions, vexed by this pollution of their sanctuary, rose in anger, but the Prophet ﷺ stopped them, bade them allow the man to finish undisturbed, then gently explain to him that his behavior was inappropriate.

01 The Bedouin are notorious for their coarse manners and lack of courtesy. This one stopped the Prophet ﷺ on his way, roughly demanding a donation. His discourtesy aroused the Companions' anger, but the Prophet ﷺ simply smiled and went on increasing his donation until the man declared himself fully satisfied.

25

RIGHTS OF THE HOUSE OF PROPHECY

No person of any consequence should revere or praise an ignorant man, even if he is of noble birth and virtuous ancestry. For to respect and praise such a person to his face may have an adverse effect on him, religiously speaking, by deceiving him as concerns God, and rendering him indifferent to good works and oblivious of gathering provisions for the Hereafter. The one who has revered and praised him will have been the cause of this temptation and illusion, and it will be as if he was trying to destroy him. He may thus deserve the wrath of God, His Messenger ﷺ and those virtuous ancestors of this ignorant man from whom he derives his nobility. How can anyone be deceived by a noble lineage in the absence of rectitude? Or depend on it when the Messenger of God—may blessings and peace be upon him and his family—had said, *O Fāṭima daughter of Muḥammad!*[01] *I can avail you naught against God!* as in the authentic *ḥadīth* where he calls, *O sons of ʿAbdal-Muṭṭalib! O so and so! calling upon his kinsmen in general, then in particular?*[02] The harm of praising the ignorant is immense and so is the temptation it subjects him to. A man once lauded another in the presence of God's Messenger ﷺ and was told, *Woe to you! You have cut your brother's throat; were he to hear this he would never succeed!*[33] And he said—may bless-

---

01 Fāṭima (d. 11 AH). Fourth and youngest daughter of the Prophet—may God's blessings and peace be upon him and his family—who declared her to be a perfect saint. She married Imām ʿAlī, from whom she had al-Ḥasan, al-Ḥusayn, Zaynab, and Umm Kūlthūm—may God be pleased with them.

02 The Prophet ﷺ addressed his tribe thus: *O sons of Kaʿb ibn Luʾayy, save yourselves from the Fire! O sons of Mūsā ibn Kaʿb, save yourselves from the Fire! O sons of ʿAbd Shams, save yourselves from the Fire! O sons of ʿAbd Manāf, save yourselves from the Fire! O sons of Hāshim, save yourselves from the Fire! O Fāṭima, save yourself from the Fire! For I can avail you naught against God. However, there are bonds of kinship between us which I shall uphold.*

ings and peace be upon him—*It is better for one of you to chase his brother with a sharp knife than to praise him to his face.*[34]

Praises and flattering remarks will harm the self-deceiving ignorant man who lacks religious perspicacity, knowledge and certitude, but not the scholar endowed with discernment and knowledge of his Lord and of himself. The Messenger of God ﷺ praised some of his Companions and others also praised them in his presence, but this only increased them in religious knowledge and discernment, and resolution and eagerness in obedience and worship. A *ḥadīth* states that, *When the believer is praised to his face, faith blossoms in his heart.*[35] However, people of discernment and good counsel to themselves are few, especially these days, while people of ignorance and delusion are many. So let believers beware, if they are God-fearing and wish to protect their religion from anything damaging to themselves or any of their brother Muslims.

When told that such and such a person, although from the House of Prophecy [*Ahl al-Bayt*], commits transgressions or mixes good with evil, some people answer that he is one of the People of the House of the Messenger of God ﷺ and that the Prophet ﷺ will intercede for them, and that perhaps their sins will cause them no harm. This is an atrocious thing to say and whoever utters such a thing harms himself and other ignorant people. How can anyone say such a thing when in the Lofty Book of God there are sufficient indications that if the People of the House are rewarded doubly for their good works, they are also punished doubly for their sins? As in God the Exalted's saying, **Wives of the Prophet! Whosoever among you commits a flagrant indecency, for her the chastisement shall be doubled.**[36] (See also the next verse.[01]) His ﷺ wives are of his House. Whoever either claims or simply thinks that neglecting obedience and committing sins are not damaging to people of noble lineage and virtuous ancestry has slandered God and gone against the Muslim consensus. However, those who belong to the House of

---

01 The full passage runs as follows: **O Prophet, say to your wives: If you desire the life of this world and its adornment, come now, I will make you provision and set you free with kindness. But if you desire God and His Messenger and the Last Abode, surely God has prepared for those amongst you that do good a mighty wage. O Wives of the Prophet! Whosoever among you commits a flagrant indecency, for her the chastisement shall be doubled; that is easy for God. But whosoever of you is obedient to God and His Messenger and works righteousness, We shall pay her wage twice over; and We have prepared for her a generous provision.** [Qur'ān, 33:28–31]

the Messenger of God ﷺ are nevertheless noble and he takes particularly good care of them. He repeatedly exhorted his community to look after them and encouraged it to love and befriend them. So, too, does God in His Book when He ﷻ says Say: **I ask for no reward from you save love for kinsfolk.**[37] Therefore, all Muslims must have love, friendship, respect, and reverence for them, without extravagance and avoiding excesses. Those among the People of the House who follow in the footsteps of their virtuous ancestors and keep to their well-pleasing way are leaders and people should be guided by their lights, and emulate their conduct, as was done with their rightly-guided forefathers. Among the latter were the earliest leaders, such as the Commander of the Faithful, Imām ʿAlī ibn Abī Ṭālib[01], al-Ḥasan[02] and al-Ḥusayn[03], the two descendants of the Messenger of God ﷺ Jaʿfar al-Ṭayyār[04], Ḥamza the Lord of Martyrs[05], ʿAbdallāh ibn ʿAbbās, the Nation's Scholar[06], his father

---

01 ʿAlī ibn Abī Ṭālib (d. 40 AH). Cousin and son-in-law of the Prophet—may God's blessings and peace be upon him and his family—being the son of his paternal uncle Abū Ṭālib and husband of his youngest daughter the Lady Fāṭima. He was also the fourth Rightly-Guided Caliph of Islam.

02 Al-Ḥasan ibn ʿAlī (d. c. 50 AH). Grandson of the Prophet—may God's blessings and peace be upon him and his family—and Imām ʿAlī's eldest son. He was the fifth Rightly-Guided Caliph and abdicated in favor of Mu'āwiya to avoid bloodshed among Muslims as foretold by the Prophet—may God's blessings and peace be upon him and his family. He spent the rest of his life in Madina until poisoned by one of his wives at the instigation of Yazīd son of Mu'āwiya and was buried in the Baqīʿ Cemetery next to his mother, the Lady Fātima.

03 Al-Ḥusayn (d. 61 AH). Grandson of the Prophet—may God's blessings and peace be upon him and his family—and Imām ʿAlī's second son. He was martyred at the hands of the Umayyad Yazīd son of Mu'āwiya's forces at Karbalā.

04 Jaʿfar ibn Abī Ṭālib, later to be known as al-Ṭayyār (d. 8 AH). ʿAlī's brother and one of the three generals who were killed in succession at the Battle of Mu'ta in present day Jordan. Soon after he died the Prophet—may God's blessings and peace be upon him and his family—who loved him very much, informed his Companions in Madina that he had seen him flying with the Angels, hence his title al-Ṭayyār, the Flyer.

05 Ḥamza (d. 3). Paternal uncle of the Prophet—may God's blessings and peace be upon him and his family—who was of approximately the same age. A true hero of Islam, he was martyred at Uḥud.

06 ʿAbdallāh ibn ʿAbbās. (d. 68), Son of al-ʿAbbās and thus cousin of the Prophet—may God's blessings and peace be upon him and his family—who had prayed for him that God should teach him the meaning of the Qur'ān and the understanding of religion. Following the death of the Prophet—may God's blessings and peace be

Imām al-ʿAbbās[01], who was the Messenger of God's uncle, Imām Zayn al-ʿAbidīn ʿAlī, the son of al-Ḥusayn[02], Imām al-Baqīr[03] and his son, Imām Jaʿfar al-Ṣādiq[04]—may peace be upon them—and those who resemble them among the early and late members of this Pure House. Those who belong to this House but do not follow the ways of their unblemished ancestors, and who, because of their ignorance, confuse things, should still be respected and revered because of their relation to the Messenger. However, those qualified to do so must never neglect to counsel them appropriately and exhort them to follow their ancestors in their knowledge, good works, gracious attributes, and satisfactory conduct. They must be told that they, of all people, are more worthy of this, and that lineage on its own can be of no benefit, nor can it elevate in the absence of *taqwā* and presence of eagerness for the world, neglect of obedience, and allowing oneself to be sullied by transgressions.

Not only have religious leaders and scholars understood this, but some poets also. One of them said,

By your life! A man is but his religion's son,
So never neglect taqwā and depend on lineage.

---

upon him and his family—he became a close disciple of Imām ʿAlī—may God be pleased with him—and one of the most important scholars among the Companions and a prolific narrator of *ḥadīth*.

01 Al-ʿAbbās ibn ʿAbdal-Muṭṭalib. (d. 32 AH) Paternal uncle of the Prophet—may God's blessings and peace be upon him and his family.

02 Imām ʿAlī ibn al-Ḥusayn, known as Zayn al-ʿAbidīn, the "Splendor of the Worshippers" (d. 93 AH) because among his devotions were one thousand *rakʿas* every night. Claimed by the Twelver Shīʿa as their fourth Imām, he was a scholar and saint of the highest order, heir to his parents' knowledge and spiritual secrets.

03 Imām Muḥammad ibn ʿAlī al-Bāqir (d. 114 AH). Grandson of Imām Ḥusayn and claimed by the Twelver Shīʿa to be their fifth Imām. He was immensely learned not only in religious sciences, but in all the sciences of his time, including astronomy and medicine, and most of the scholars of his time, both Sunnī and Shīʿa, benefitted from him.

04 Imām Jaʿfar ibn Muḥammad al-Ṣādiq (d. 148 AH). Descendent of Imām Ḥusayn and claimed by the Twelver Shīʿa to be their sixth Imām, he was a man of encyclopedic knowledge and supreme sanctity. Numerous eminent scholars learned from him in Madina where he lived and died, including Imām Mālik, Imām Abū Ḥanīfa, and others.

For Islam exalted the Persian Salmān[01]
While idolatry abased the noble Abū Lahab.[02]

And al-Mutanabbī said,

If the soul of a nobleman is not as noble as his ancestry
What good will a distinguished position do him?

Another poet said,

Of what use is Hāshimite lineage
If the soul hails from Bāhila?[03]

The same applies to the descendants of saintly people. When they follow in their ancestors' footsteps, they are equally virtuous and deserve to be revered and have their blessings sought. When, on the other hand, they are ignorant and heedless, they must be counseled and guided to the right way. Nevertheless, they should be given a certain amount of respect for their ancestors' sakes; why should they not when God the Exalted says about the two boys and the wall, **And underneath it was a treasure belonging to them, and their father had been virtuous.**[04] It was said that this refers to their seventh ancestor on their mother's side. For his sake, they were protected in their worldly affairs, let alone those of their Hereafter. Know this, understand, place everything in its place, give each his due, seek God's help and you will be happy and rightly-guided! The matter is entirely God's.

---

01 Salmān al Fārisī (d. 36 AH). Persian Companion the Prophet—may God's blessings and peace be upon him and his family—who had been sold into slavery in Syria and brought to Madina where the Prophet—may God's blessings and peace be upon him and his family—helped him buy his freedom.

02 Abū Lahab, (d. 2 AH). Paternal uncle of the Prophet—may God's blessings and peace be upon him and his family—who refused to accept Islam, became a hardened disbeliever, and one of the leaders of the Meccan persecution against the early believing community.

03 Bāhila is a tribe which was considered of lower rank than most other tribes.

04 Qur'ān, 18:82. The reference is to the story of the two orphans in *Sūrat al-Kahf* and how God instructed *Sayyidunā* al-Khidr to protect their treasure for them by repairing the wall that was threatening to crumble and expose the treasure. According to the commentaries, their virtuous ancestor for whose sake this was done was their seventh maternal ancestor. This is a clear indication to how powerful and influential the *baraka* of a saintly ancestor may be.

26

ASSESSING ONE'S SPIRITUAL STATE

Should a person wish to know whether in religious terms he is improving and ascending or diminishing and descending, he should look at how his state and conduct had been in the month that has just gone by or the year that has just ended. If he finds that they were better in his estimation and superior to his present state and conduct, let him know that he is falling into degradation; whereas if he finds his present state and conduct better and superior to his previous ones, let him know that he is ascending and improving. It has been handed down that, *He who finds his day to resemble the day before has been cheated, and he who finds his day to be worse than the day before is accursed.*[01] 'Accursed' here means remote from a particular and specially accorded mercy. He who is not increasing is diminishing. To elaborate: if, when thinking about previous days you feel that you then had no wish for the world, were eager for the Hereafter, scrupulously avoided doubtful things, were quick to good actions, prompt in obedience, and remote from transgressions, and by comparison are now no better or to any extent worse, then know that you are going down, deteriorating in your religion, your aspiration for God, and in your striving for the Hereafter. You should then feel apprehensive and fearful, and begin to move resolutely forward and exert effort. If, on the other hand, you find that you have more aspiration and eagerness than before, then thank God the Exalted even

01 Daylamī, *Musnad al-Firdaws*, 5910, on the authority of 'Alī ibn Abī Ṭālib transmitting it from the Prophet—may God's blessings and peace be upon him; Qāḍī Abū Bakr ibn Muḥammad al-Anṣārī, *al-Shuyūkh al-Thiqāt*, 322. The chain of transmission of this *ḥadīth* is considered very weak and this is why the Imām introduces it by saying, "it has been handed down", and not categorically, as in "The Messenger of God—may God's blessings and peace be upon him—has said".

more so, remember His gifts and graciousness, and be ever-attentive to them. You should never feel pleased with yourself, nor think that it is due to your own ability and power, for as God the Exalted has said, **Had it not been for the favor of God upon you and His mercy, not one of you would ever have been purified; but God purifies whom He wills, and God is the Hearing, the Knowing.**[38]

27

ATTENDING TO THE REQUIREMENTS OF THIS WORLD AND THOSE OF THE NEXT

Anyone who accords his worldly life and his life-to-come equal attention, inwardly shows them the same degree of concentration and eagerness, and outwardly exhibits for both an equal amount of effort and serious pursuit, is excessively foolish and unreservedly stupid. What then of anyone who gives more attention and effort to his worldly life? And what then of anyone who pays no attention at all, nor exerts any effort for his life-to-come? We ask God to guard us against this and all other afflictions and dangers, and to guard our loved ones and all Muslims!

Those who give their worldly life and their life-to-come equal attention deserve to be described as foolish and stupid as stated above because they do not differentiate between that which is better, more permanent, purer and more spacious, and that which is lowly, ephemeral, turbid, disturbing and narrow. They are thus similar or even stranger and more extraordinary than those who treat equally diamonds and dung, or pure gold and clay. Had the life-to-come nothing to its credit but perpetuity and freedom from flaws, these should suffice for it to be given superiority and priority. As one of our Virtuous Predecessors once said—may God have mercy on them—'Had the world been made of perishable gold and the Hereafter of permanent clay, we should prefer permanent clay to perishable gold. What then when the reality is the reverse?'

It is evident that those who prefer this world to the Hereafter are doubt-ridden suspicious people, while those who treat them equally are unintelligent fools, and only those who prefer the Hereafter are intelligent, resolute believers.

All blessings are God's. He bestows His favors upon whom He wills. Guidance is God's, He guides whom He wills. He is the Wise, the Knowing.

28

AILMENTS OF THE HEART

Ailments of the heart are, in many ways and from many different points of view, more harmful, dangerous, repugnant, and hideous, than those of the body. Most harmful and dangerous is the fact that the ailments of the heart affect a man's religion—which is his capital for happiness in this world and the Next—and damage his life-to-come, which is the life of permanence and eternity. Physical illness, on the other hand, damages a man's worldly life, which is ephemeral and quick to end, and his body, which is a target for afflictions and rapid destruction. Furthermore, physical illness may be of great benefit to one's religion and to one's future life, for God has made great rewards and numerous immediate and delayed benefits the consequences of illness, as is evident from numerous Qur'ānic verses and *ḥadīths* detailing the rewards attached to illnesses and afflictions of the body.

Since the ailments of the heart cannot be perceived by the senses and yield no painful physical symptoms, they are hidden and difficult to recognize and study, and people have come to pay little heed to them and no longer seek to have them treated and cured. Such people are, as Imām al-Ghazālī—may God be pleased with him—says, like he who is disfigured by vitiligo[01], but possesses no mirror. When another person informs him of his affliction, he does not believe him. Furthermore, the pains and punishments that await those whose hearts are diseased in the Hereafter are perceived as unlikely by the heedless, something exceedingly remote. They may even have doubts about their very existence—may God protect

01 Vitiligo is a skin disease leading to discoloration of skin patches of various sizes. It was frequently confused with leprosy in ancient times, but there are two distinct terms for these in Arabic, *Baraṣ* for Vitiligo, and *Judhām* for Leprosy.

us—or they may deceive themselves with false hopes and illusions about God, promising themselves that they will be forgiven and saved without having to work for it, and thus arouse in themselves the expectation that they will end up safe and secure. Because of these and similar attitudes, the ailments of the heart remain veiled and become overpowering. The heedless make light of them, and people no longer look for remedies, to the extent that some may be well aware of one or more diseases in their hearts, yet carry on quite unperturbed. By contrast, should they feel or be informed of a disease in their bodies, they are most concerned and worried, keen to have it treated, and ready to go to the very limits of their resources to do so. The reason behind this is that, as we have stated above, diseases of the heart cannot be grasped by the senses, yield no physical pain, and the punishments they entail are not in evidence here and now, since they occur only after death in the Hereafter. The heedless think of death as remote and regard what follows it is as even farther away. Were they only to employ their intelligence and seek certitude they would know that death is the nearest of hidden things lying in wait, as he has said—may blessings and peace be upon him.[01] He also said—may blessings and peace be upon him, *The Garden is nearer to you than the laces of your sandals and so is the Fire.*[39]

The ailments of the heart are many and one of the most dangerous and harmful is to harbor doubts about religion—may God protect us! Others include weakness of faith in God, His Messenger and the Hereafter, ostentatiously flaunting one's acts of worship, arrogance towards God's servants, greed, avarice, jealousy, rancor, deceiving other Muslims, loving the world and being preoccupied with it, harboring long hopes and forgetting death, being heedless of the Hereafter and neglecting to work for it, and so on. Since hearts are imperceptible to the senses and their ailments produce no outwardly detectable pain, it is necessary for any intelligent man, anxious for his religion and safety in the life-to-come, to eagerly search for the ailments hidden in his heart, strive to identify them, and begin to treat and remedy them before death suddenly overtakes him and he returns to his Lord, only to meet Him with an unsound heart. He might then be one of the losers and perish along with those who will perish.

---

01 This is frequently quoted by scholars and Sufis but nowhere is it attributed to the Prophet—may God's blessings and peace be upon him and his family—by a regular chain of transmission.

The heart's ailments can be identified by recognizing the outward signs that indicate their existence. These are numerous and the most evident are: laziness with respect to acts of obedience, sluggishness in good works, greed for the world's pleasures and passions, eagerness for worldly prosperity, yearning to live long in this world, and other similar attributes of the heedless and of those who turn away from God the Exalted. When these signs of the heart's sickness are detected, one must strive to treat them. The shortest and most effective way is to search for a Shaykh who is a Knower and a scholar, one of the 'people of hearts and secrets'. Should he fail to find such a one, let him take counsel from a virtuous brother of good counsel who can help in the identification and treatment of these ailments. Should he fail to find such a brother, as is generally the case in these days when so few people help one another in truth and virtue, then he must resort to the books of the leading authorities in such matters, where the diseases and their remedies are described. The most comprehensive and useful of these is *Iḥyā 'Ulūm al-Dīn* (*Revival of the Religious Sciences*), especially the volume on 'Mortal Vices', for the book was written for the express purpose of recognizing the ailments of the heart, the signs indicating their existence, how strong or weak they are, and the methods with which to treat them. Books are not, however, a substitute for a Shaykh who is a Knower, or a virtuous brother; they should be a last resort for those unable to find either. God the Exalted helps the seeker according to his determination, sincerity, and aspiration; and He—Transcendent is He—is the Patron and Helper.

29

THE BALANCE BETWEEN GOOD AND EVIL ACTS

He who is either unable or lacks the energy to perform all possible good works should not, for those reasons, abandon them all, but should engage in whatever is easy and accessible. For goodness attracts goodness, small acts of goodness attract great ones, a little invites plenty, and, as has been handed down, *Goodness is a habit.*[40] Similarly, he who is incapable of abandoning all evil must abandon whatever of it he can, for a mixture of good and evil is better and lighter than total evil. Good works erase sins, as in the *ḥadīth*, *Follow a sin with an act of goodness and it will erase it.*[41] And in another, *If you commit a sin, follow it up with an act of goodness and it will requite it; hidden sins with hidden acts of goodness; public with public.*[42] A servant afflicted with evil and transgressions must never altogether turn away from God, nor from good works and obedience, for otherwise there will remain between him and his Lord no avenue for reconciliation or for returning to Him. Let him heed the lesson in the story of the highwayman who shed blood and robbed Muslims of their money. A virtuous man once saw him do these things while fasting. He asked him, 'How can you do what you are doing and yet fast?' The man replied, 'Yes! I am leaving open a channel for reconciliation and will not sever all links between myself and my Lord.' Sometime later he saw the brigand ambling around the Kaʿba, having repented, and was told by him, 'That fasting reconciled me with my Lord.'

It is now evident that a Muslim should maintain a state of entire goodness and complete obedience. However, if this is not possible, if he is being hindered by his ego and its appetites, and this leads him into any manner of evil or sin, then he must firmly preserve those acts of obedience which he finds possible and easy.

And God is the Patron, the Praiseworthy.

30

THE COMPANY ONE KEEPS

The company one keeps and the people one spends time and mixes with have major effects which bring on either benefit and improvement, or harm and corruption, depending on whether the company is that of virtuous and superior people, or depraved and evil ones. These effects may not appear suddenly, but as a gradual process that unfolds after prolonged contact with either kind of people. The Messenger of God—may blessings and peace be upon him—said, *A man is with those he loves.*[43] And, *A man's religion is that of his intimates, so let each of you be careful whom he becomes intimate with.*[44] And, *A virtuous companion is like the merchant of musk; either he will offer you some, or you will buy it from him, or you will find there a pleasant smell. An evil companion, on the other hand, is like the bellows-blower; either he will scorch your clothes, or you will smell its stench.*[45] If you wish to know whether those you mix and sit with increase or diminish your faith, religion and works, examine your faith, religion, good character, praiseworthy intentions, and power of resolution in performing acts of obedience and goodness before getting to know them. Then keep their company and mix with them and see: if you find that the above mentioned things have intensified and become more deeply ingrained, and that you have become more desirous and interested in them, then know that this particular company is of benefit to your religion and your heart, and that if you continue and persevere with it you will gain even greater benefits and acquire many more good things, God willing. If, on the other hand, you find that your religion has grown weaker and shakier, know that this company is harmful, that its harm to your religion and your heart is evident, and that if you continue with it, it will lead to even greater harm and evil, may God protect us! You should also examine the bad points you had before and after keeping that company. This is the way to evaluate one's position vis-à-vis those with whom one mixes and takes for companions. The decisive factor here is whether good or evil is more powerful and predominant. When goodness in that company is more powerful and predominant, then a wicked man who mixes with them may become attracted to goodness and its people; whereas when wickedness prevails and dominates, then it is to be feared that the good people who keep such company may become attracted to wickedness and its people.

These are subtle concepts known to people of discernment and experience in such matters. To explain them in detail needs much elaboration. He said—may blessings and peace be upon him—*A good companion is better than solitude, and solitude is better than a wicked companion.*[46] He was given—may blessings and peace be upon him—a conciseness of expression that no other man, whether of ancient or recent times, was ever given.

31

THE REPUTATION OF MEN AND THE PROBLEMS OF POWER

Close contact with a God-fearing believer proves him better than his reputation, however good it may be. The more you mix, get to know, and deal with him, the more your affection and respect for him grow, because of what you are able to observe at close range of his attentiveness to God, respect for His injunctions, swiftness to act for His good pleasure, perseverance in obedience, avoidance of sins, and being vigilant and on his guard against anything likely to attract God's wrath. By contrast, close contact with a depraved hypocrite proves him worse than his reputation, however odious it may already be. The more you experience and mix with him, the more you loathe and detest him, because of his neglect of God's injunctions, swiftness to perform activities loathsome to Him, sluggishness in obedience, and carelessness with his obligations to God. The foregoing makes it clear that getting to know the believer proves him better than what is said about him, while getting to know the hypocrite is the opposite.

Not very far from this is the situation of people in high positions, either of religion, such as scholars and people of virtue, or of the world, such as kings and rulers. When the people nearest and most connected to them are good and righteous, this indicates their own goodness, righteousness, and good management of their affairs. However, some of the people connected with them, but separated by a distance, may not be as we have just described. This means that those in power either display a certain amount of weakness in the performance of their duties, or, being too preoccupied with other things of lesser importance, are unaware [of what their own officials do]. Thus, the better and more upright those near to them are and the worse those remote from them, the more this indicates that they themselves are good and righteous, but weak in fulfilling their duties, or are unobservant and careless in seeking information about things for which he is responsible. Another possible reason is that areas of authority may grow larger and the subjects more numerous and spread out. Such a situation was referred to by the words of the Commander of the Faithful, ʿUmar ibn al-Khaṭṭāb[01]—may God be pleased with him—when he said in the last days of his caliphate, 'O Lord God! I have aged and grown weaker, and my subjects have spread abroad. Take me to You without me having succumbed to temptation or neglect.' He also said, 'Should a lamb die of neglect on the banks of the Euphrates, I would fear being called to account for it.'

It is thus clear that those who either are afflicted by some weakness, or lack the ability to observe and investigate adequately cannot adequately shoulder high positions and large responsibilities. This is perhaps why some of the greatest men of religion have backed away and fled from such positions, preferring safety, which is one of the two gains[02]. As he said—may blessings and peace be upon him—*A soul to whom you give life is better than a governorship that you cannot control,*[03] meaning: for which you are incapable of adequately assuming responsibility.

And God—Transcendent is He—knows best.

---

01 ʿUmar ibn al-Khaṭṭāb (d. 23 AH). Eminent Companion, second Rightly-Guided Caliph, and father-in-law of the Prophet—may God's blessings and peace be upon him and his family. Known as *al-Fārūq*, "The Discriminator", for his trenchant ability to discriminate between right and wrong.

02 See footnote 46

03 Abū Nuʿaym, *Ḥilyat al-Awliyā*, 6:138. To refrain from actively seeking a position of power is to give life to one's soul by saving it from the arrogance, conceit, injustice, and other perils associated with such offices.

32

KEEPING COMPANY WITH THE VIRTUOUS

It is desirable and recommended to associate, keep company, and mix with those people of religion and goodness who are the scholars who practice what they know and the virtuous servants of God. This has many benefits, both immediate and deferred, and there are numerous *ḥadīths* and other traditions detailing them. However, people who desire and eagerly seek such things differ greatly in their aims. The first and highest aim in keeping company and associating with such people is to study their sciences, learn their courtesy, and observe their good character, praiseworthy qualities, good works and speech, so as to emulate them and drive oneself single-mindedly toward acquiring their good character and engaging in their good works. One should associate with them for these reasons to the exclusion of all others.

Others keep their company out of love for them, because they prefer God's religion over all else, establish His ordinances, occupy themselves with His obedience, and strive to draw nearer to Him by the acquisition of useful knowledge and good character, and doing good works. They love them for this and wish to associate with them to try to emulate them and drive their souls to imitate their good works and acquire their good character, but only as time and circumstances permit. When they miss some of those things they are sorry and wish they had succeeded in doing them. A *ḥadīth* says, *A man is with those he loves.*[47] Another says, *He who emulates certain people becomes one of them.*[48]

Still others associate with them to benefit from their *baraka* and good prayers, but have neither the intention nor the determination to follow their example and emulate their pattern. This is not devoid of *baraka* and goodness and is alluded to in the *ḥadīth Qudsī* which ends, '*They are the people whose companions never suffer wretchedness'.*[01] This even applies to those who associate with them in order to be protected through the good fortune and *baraka* of their company from the iniquitous and aggressive among human and jinn demons. These will never be disappointed, nor will the *baraka* be withheld from them. They will be withheld, however, from those whose aim is to acquire a reputation among people for keeping such company, hoping thus to be able to attain to prohibited and illicit things, thinking wrongly that if people know them to associate with the good and virtuous they will never suspect them of illegal practices and forbidden actions. It is not impossible for some who are forsaken by God and the object of His anger to harbor such aims. In the chapter detailing the different kinds of ostentation and their goals, the Proof of Islam ﵁ says that some parade their acts of obedience so that people may know about them, which makes it possible for them to behave with depravity. If this is possible as concerns acts of obedience, it is equally possible as concerns mixing with the virtuous. The Devil is a manifest enemy, and he uses numerous kinds of deceitful and fraudulent stratagems among which are these. There are more dangerous, reprehensible, evil and harmful things still. We ask God for wellbeing and protection, for He is the Best of Protectors.

---

01 Muslim, *Ṣaḥīḥ*, 2689. The *ḥadīth* runs as follows: *God has Angels who roam the streets, searching for the people of Remembrance. When they find people engaged in the Remembrance of God, they call to each other, saying "Come to your task!" and they spread their wings around them as high as the Terrestrial Heaven. Then their Lord asks them—although He has more knowledge then they—"What are My slaves saying?" And they reply, "They are extolling, magnifying, praising, and glorifying You." "Have they seen Me?" He asks, and they say, "No, by God, they have not seen You." He then says, "How would it be, then, had they seen Me?" "Had they seen You," the Angels reply, "they would have worshipped and glorified You more intensely, and extolled You even more abundantly." He then asks, "What are they asking for?" and they reply, "They are asking You for the Garden." He says, "Have they seen it?" and they answer "No, by God, they have not seen it, O Lord!" "What if they had seen it?" He asks, and they say, "Had they seen it, they would have been more intent on winning it, more ardent in asking for it, and they would have yearned for it even more intensely." He then asks, "What are they seeking protection from?" and they reply, "They seek protection from the Fire." He says: "Have they seen it?" and they answer, "No, by God, they have not seen it." He asks: "What if they had seen it?" "Had they seen it," they reply, "they would have been even more fearful and more determined to flee from it." He then says, "I call you to witness that I have forgiven them!" One of the Angels then says, "O Lord! So-and-so is among them, a sinful servant who was just passing by and joined them." And He declares, "And him too have I forgiven; they are the people whose companions never suffer wretchedness."*

33

THE DEGREES OF ḤALĀL AND ḤARĀM

It is an obligation, after the other known obligations, that one should seek *ḥalāl* things. Eating *ḥalāl* food and wearing *ḥalāl* clothes, while confining oneself to that necessary to fulfil one's needs, have great advantages, beautiful results, numerous benefits, and bring to fruition momentous and precious things. Such is indispensable if one is to clean and purify one's heart, render it more subtle and illuminated, adorn it with noble upright beliefs, saving qualities and good character, and purify one's senses with good works, sincere obedience and upright speech.

Legally permitted, or *ḥalāl,* things are of many degrees; the highest and best being that which is absolutely *ḥalāl* and retains its originally permissible quality[01] in every respect. Such is sweet running water, herbs growing on uncultivated land, hunted game and fish from the sea that are edible and sufficient. These are entirely *ḥalāl* when eaten in the legally permitted way, with due caution, and with the God-fearing intention of using them as assistance in obeying God, worshipping Him, and establishing His rule, and in quantities not exceeding the strictly necessary. Some of the Virtuous Predecessors [*salaf*]—may God have mercy on them—ate only herbs for so long that their bodies began to turn greenish. As for Sufyān al-Thawrī[02] and Ibrāhīm ibn Adham[03]—may God have mercy on them—when they found no *ḥalāl* of that description they simply ate sand; for them it was sufficiently nutritious to replace food. There are herbs growing on some

---

01 The legal rule according to the Sacred Law is that everything is inherently *ḥalāl*, the few things legally forbidden beings the exception. Thus, anything about which no legal interdiction exists is *ḥalāl*. Being permissible is the original essential quality of all things, while being forbidden is accidental.

02 Sufyān al-Thawrī (d. 161 AH) Great scholar, jurist, and transmitter of *ḥadīth*.

03 See footnote 48.

mountains and valleys which a man can eat and nothing else besides. God supports the servant according to his intention and aim.

The second degree of *ḥalāl* is that which is pure, entirely *ḥalāl* in one respect, but not in another, for instance, food and clothes bought in strictly necessary quantities with money earned by selling herbs and wood gathered from the valleys, with due scrupulousness. Some of our Virtuous Predecessors have done this.

The third degree is that which is obtained when the thing is absolutely *ḥalāl* in neither of these respects but acquired with money earned as a merchant or a craftsman; a silversmith, for example, or a tailor. This degree of *ḥalāl* exists when these people buy and sell, while maintaining *taqwā*, scrupulousness, vigilance, and caution, and with the good intention of using that which they earn to assist them in God's obedience, in conforming to His injunctions, using nothing but the strictly necessary to fulfil their needs in the way of food, clothes, and other requirements, and giving the surplus away in charitable and benevolent acts done solely for the sake of God the Exalted.

The fourth degree of *ḥalāl* applies to those people whose actions are mixed, who are neither cautious in their transactions, nor keen to avoid dubious things. They are complacent, and show little *taqwā* in whatever they take or leave. Thus, much of their money is of dubious provenance, and their possessions represent a mixture. About them it is said, 'Whoever cares not where he obtains his money, God cares not from which of the gates of Hell He will make him enter.'

These are the four degrees of *ḥalāl* opposed to which are another four degrees representing things which are either *ḥarām* or altogether prohibited, restricted, dubious, or problematic.

The first of these is that which is altogether prohibited, except in the case of dire necessity. Examples of this category include carrion, blood, pork, and alcohol.

The second category is made of things which are *ḥalāl* in themselves, but forbidden because owned by someone else. Barley, wheat, dates and raisins could be examples. These are *ḥarām* unless they reach you licitly through either purchase, gift, or inheritance.

The third category consists of such items which are either originally *ḥarām* but have become *ḥalāl* through dubious means, unacceptable to people of truth and *taqwā* who do not depend on such things, but accepted promptly by those of little knowledge and *taqwā* who are overcome by their egos and passions. Of this category, also are those things which were originally *ḥalāl* until doubts were raised as to whether for some reason they have become *ḥarām*. There is a sound *ḥadīth* which states, *Those who fall into doubtful things will fall into the prohibited. Like the shepherd who grazes his animals near the edge of the interdicted area and is therefore likely to trespass into it.*[49] There is also the well known *ḥadīth* of 'Uqba, who once married a woman, after which a black woman came along and claimed that she had breastfed both of them.[01] There are many examples illustrating this category and the Proof of Islam ☙ has written on this at great length in the section on *ḥalāl* and *ḥarām* in the *Ihya*.

As for problematic things, they are mostly *ḥalāl* in appearance, but to accept them necessitates complacency, carelessness as to whom one deals with or takes from, wastefulness, overspending, excess and pleasure seeking. This is where the *ḥalāl* becomes narrow and people take risks in what they use, how they transact business, and the pleasures and comforts they pursue. It is said that *ḥalāl* does not bear wastefulness. A *ḥadīth* states, *A servant does not reach the degree of the people of taqwā until he leaves that which is untainted for fear of that which is tainted.*[50] And one of the Companions—may God be pleased with them all—said, 'We used to leave nine-tenths of what was licit for fear of falling into the prohibited.' And a *ḥadīth* narrated by al-Ḥasan, son of 'Alī—may God be pleased with both—says, *Leave that which arouses your suspicion for that which does not.*[51]

And God knows best.

---

01 Bukhārī, *Ṣaḥīḥ*, 2659. When 'Uqba reported what, the woman had said to the Messenger of God—may blessings and peace be upon him and his family—he told him to divorce her because of the doubts that had been raised over the legality of his marriage.

34

THE INSINUATIONS OF THE DEVIL

Among the most harmful things that can befall a person as he prays, recites the Qur'ān, or invokes God the Exalted, are the whisperings in the breast, the crowding of thoughts, and the ego's prattling about matters past and future. When the heart is submerged in these and preoccupied with them, they ruin the essence, meaning, and aim of his devotional activities and may even ruin their outward appearance as well. His state will then equal that of one who has not performed them at all, or even worse. This will be familiar to he who is concerned with and has experience in these matters, who is concerned for his religion, giving his Lord what is due to Him, and working for his life-to-come.

When these thoughts and prattling concern acts of obedience unrelated to the matter at hand, they are but satanic plots and attempts to confuse the believer by selling him evil dressed up as good. If they concern barely licit things, then this is even baser and more villainous; whereas if they are to do with sins and rebellions, this is the worst and ugliest of all. These latter may cause a servant to be expelled from the Presence of God the Exalted, thus becoming a loathsome repudiate. So, let the servant beware of this to the utmost; let him not abandon his soul to its prattling and fruitless whisperings when standing before God the Exalted, remembering Him, communing with Him, praying before His Face, or reciting His sublime Book.

He who strives, strives only for himself, for indeed God has no need of the worlds.[52] **But none are granted it save those who are steadfast, and none is granted it save he who is immensely fortunate; and if an insinuation from the Devil reaches you, seek refuge in God; He is indeed the Hearing, the Knowing.**[53]

35

RECTITUDE

Rectitude or uprightness [*istiqāma*] on the Straight Path, the even road leading to God the Exalted, which is devoid of crookedness and deviation, is most difficult, nearly unattainable, save for the Prophets, who are infallible, and for the great people of God, the *Ṣiddīqūn* among the well-guarded saints.

God the Exalted has said to His trustworthy Messenger, **Be upright as you were commanded, and those who turn [to God] with you, and transgress not, for He sees what you do; up until, And endure patiently, for God wastes not the reward of those who excel.**[01] And He ﷻ says **and be upright as you were commanded, and follow not their whims, and say, I believe in whatever Book God has sent down, up until, and to Him is the becoming!**[02] And He ﷻ says **Those who say, 'Our Lord is God' then are upright, the angels descend upon them. . . up until, A gift of welcome from One Forgiving, Compassionate."**[03] And He ﷻ says **Those who say, 'Our**

---

01 Qur'ān, 11:112–5. The full passage runs as follows: **Have rectitude as you were commanded, and those who turn [to God] with you, and transgress not, for He sees what you do; and incline not toward those who do wrong lest the Fire touch you. You have no ally against God, nor will you be supported. Establish the Prayer at the ends of the day and a part of the night: assuredly, good deeds banish evil ones. This is a reminder for the mindful. And have fortitude, for God wastes not the reward of those who excel.**

02 Qur'ān, 42:15. The full passage runs as follows: **To this then summon, and have rectitude as you were commanded, and follow not their whims, and say, I believe in whatever Book God has sent down, I am commanded to be just among you, God is our Lord and your Lord, to us our works and to you your works. No argument between us and you; God will bring us together, and to Him is the becoming!**

03 Qur'ān, 41:30–2. The full passage runs as follows: **Those who say, 'Our Lord is God' then are upright, the angels descend upon them saying, "Fear not nor grieve, but rejoice at the tidings of the Garden which you were promised. We are your allies in the life of the world and in the Hereafter. There you shall have what your souls**

Lord is God' then are upright, no fear shall befall them, neither shall they grieve. Those are the people of the Garden, immortal therein, as a reward for what they used to do.[54]

The Messenger of God ﷺ said, *Be upright! You will not be capable fully to achieve it.*[55] *Aim well and as near the mark as you can, and know that none will be saved by virtue of his works.* "Not even you, O Messenger of God?" they asked, and he answered, *Not even I, were it not that God enfold me with mercy and grace from Him.*[56]

Sufyān ibn 'Abdallāh[01]—may God be pleased with him—said, 'I said, "O Messenger of God! Tell me something about Islam such that I need ask no-one else".' He answered, '*Say: I believe in God! Then be upright.*'[57] And 'Umar—may God be pleased with him—said, 'Be upright and do not swerve like a fox.'

Rectitude is the all-inclusive quality that embraces all useful knowledge, good character, and good deeds, along with even firmness, absence of wavering, disturbance, deviation or deviousness. One of our Predecessors said, 'The all-inclusive *karāma* is rectitude [*istiqāma*].' A man of virtue once saw in a dream the Messenger of God ﷺ and said to him, 'O Messenger of God! When it was said to you: "Your hair has turned grey, O Messenger of God!" "It is Hūd and its sisters that have made my hair turn grey." What is it in them that did this?' And he replied—may peace and blessings be upon him—'His saying—Exalted is He—**Be upright as you were commanded.**'[02] The *ḥadīths* which state that Hūd and its sisters turned his hair grey indicate that they did so because they spoke of the destruction of nations. **So away with the folk of Hūd! So away with Thamūd! So away with Madyan!**[03] These

---

desired, and there you shall have that for which you pray. A gift of welcome from One Forgiving, Compassionate."

01 Sufyān ibn 'Abdallāh al-Thaqafī (date of death unknown). Governed Taif during 'Umar's caliphate from 16 to 23 AH.

02 *Sūra* Hūd and its sisters are those chapters wherein the vengeance wrought on previous nations who had rejected their Messengers is described most vividly. The *ḥadīth* in question runs thus: 'Hūd and its sisters have turned my hair grey; *al-Wāqi'a*, *al-Ḥāqqa*, *al-Shams*, and *Sa'ala Sāil*.' These *sūra's* (11, 56, 69, 91, 70) aroused the Prophet's fears for those among the Arabs who were slow to accept Islam

03 Qur'ān, 11:60, 68, 95. 'Ad and Thamūd were tribes of Arabia. The first dwelt in the valley of al-Aḥqāf in Ḥadramawt, and their prophet was Hūd—may peace be upon him—whose grave is still there to be visited. The second dwelt in al-Ḥijr, a location

are not incompatible with the dream mentioned; each has an appropriate interpretation at its level. However, a soundly transmitted *ḥadīth* has a higher and more perfect standing than a dream, even though the dream be a righteous one dreamt by a righteous man.

---

about midway between Madina and Tabūk. Their prophet was Ṣāliḥ—may peace be upon him. The third, Madyan, dwelt near the Gulf of ʿAqaba. Their Prophet was Shuʿayb—may peace be upon him. All three tribes were destroyed suddenly and entirely by the wrath of God for their iniquitous dealings with each other and with strangers, and for rejecting the Divine Message conveyed to them by their Prophets. Only the Prophets and their followers escaped destruction.

36

CERTITUDE AND DETACHMENT

God says—and the mightiest and most noble of speakers is He—**In the name of God, Most Merciful and Compassionate. Alif. Lām. Mīm. This is the Book, about this there is no doubt, a guidance for those who have taqwā**, up until, **and it is they that are successful.**[01] And He ﷻ says **That Last Abode: We assign it to those who seek not exaltation on the earth, nor corruption; and the sequel is for those who have taqwā.**[58] And He ﷻ says **He who desires the harvest of the Hereafter, We increase him in its harvest, and he who desires the harvest of this world, We give him of it, but of the Hereafter he has no share.**[59]

And he said ﷺ *The sagacious is he who accuses his own soul and works for what comes after death; while the incapable is he who follows his soul's passions and indulges in [illusory] hopes [concerning] God.*[60] And he said—may blessings and peace be upon him and his family—to 'Abdallāh ibn 'Umar—may God be pleased with both—*Be in the world as a stranger or a passer-by, and count yourself among the people of the graves.*[61]

When the following verse was revealed, **Is he whose breast God has expanded for Islam, so that he follows a light from his Lord,**[62] they asked him—may blessings and peace be upon him—what this 'expansion' was, and he replied, *Light—when it enters the heart, the breast expands for it and enlarges.* They then asked whether there were signs for this and he replied,

---

01 Qur'ān, 2:1–5. The full passage runs as follows, ***Alif. Lām. Mīm.* This is the Book, about this there is no doubt, a guidance for those who have *taqwā*, believe in the Unseen, establish prayer, and spend of that which We have bestowed upon them; and those who believe in that which is revealed to you and that which was revealed before you, and are certain of the Hereafter. It is they that are upon guidance from their Lord, and it is they that are successful.**

To shun the Abode of illusion and attend to the Abode of permanence, and to prepare for death before it occurs.[63]

Those who reflect on these noble verses and sound Prophetic *ḥadīths*, along with the other verses of the August Book that elaborate on the same concept, Prophetic traditions and sayings of the Virtuous Predecessors—may God's mercy be on them all—who are the great among the Companions, Followers, or those who followed them with excellence and possessed certitude about God, His Messenger, the Last Day with its promises, threats, painful punishment for the unbelievers and the depraved, and permanent happiness in the Garden of Bliss for the people of *taqwā*, certainty, and excellence; those will lose all desire for the world's cheap possessions and ephemeral, confusing and disturbing pleasures. They will experience great longing for the Permanent Abode where bliss is perpetual and free from all blemishes and disturbances. They will be diligent, strive seriously, and devote all of their time, breaths, states, movement and stillness to that which will save them from God's wrath and punishment and be of advantage to them in the life-to-come. They will abstain from all that is worldly, except what is strictly necessary to enable them to devote themselves to acquiring useful sciences, a superior character, and good works, in order to attain their goal. They will abstain from sharing in or competing for the pleasures, appetites and passions which are pursued by the heedless and the unaware, who resemble sheep and cattle, and about whom God the Exalted says, **Those are like cattle, they are even worse, those are the heedless.**[64] They will be as Imām al-Shāfiʿī[01]—may God's mercy be upon him—says,

If you know not this world, I do; both sweet and bitter were mine.
Nothing but putrid carrion it is, surrounded by dogs, quarrelling over it.
Avoid it and be peace to its people; pull and its dogs will pull back.

Another poet says,

The intelligent test the world and see it as an enemy in friendly clothes.

Yet another says,

01 Imām Muḥammad ibn Idrīs al-Shāfiʿī (d. 204 AH). Independent Jurist, founder of one of the four canonical schools of Islamic law and of the science of the Principles of Jurisprudence.

Move away from dunyā; seek not to wed her;
Seek not to wed she who slays her spouse.
The favors you hope from her never match the anguish;
Observe and you will see how its vexations prevail.

In sum, the person of intelligence, perspicacity, and resolution is he who dedicates most of his time to preparing for his life-to-come and gathering provisions for the appointed time. He should not allot time for other things save those that are necessary to help him along, and he should do so with caution and frugality, using worldly things sparingly, and listening attentively to the words of his Prophet ﷺ who said, *What have I to do with the world? With regard to this world, I am like a rider moving on a summer day who rests under a tree, then departs and leaves it.*[65] And, *Had the world weighed with God so much as the wing of a gnat, he would not have given a disbeliever a sip of its water.*[66] And, *The world is the prison of the believer and the Garden of the disbeliever.*[67]

It is God who grants success; He is the Ally and Helper.

37

THE WORLD IS BUT A MOMENT

Imām al-Shāfiʿī—may God's mercy and good pleasure be upon him—said, 'The world is but a moment; so make it [a moment] of obedience.'

Al-Bustī[01] says in his famous poem,

Increase in worldly things is to a man but diminishment;
And his profits in other than sheer goodness are but loss.

Imām Ismāʿīl ibn al-Muqrī[02] says in the poem where he counsels his son,

Till when will you dwell in illusion and distraction;
How long will you sleep and not awaken?
Will you spend all this in the love of that
Which God set lower than the wing of a gnat?
If Qārūn's[03] *fortune from it you should obtain,*
It would still be but a morsel in your mouth and a cloth.

It is evident from everything we have mentioned in this and the previous chapter that an intelligent man possessed of certainty, wisdom and discernment should be preoccupied solely with his life-to-come and with working for it, and with that which is strictly necessary in his daily life to help him achieve his aim in the manner detailed in the previous chapter. **The one who strives, strives only for himself, for God is surely Independent**

01 Abu'l-Fatḥ ʿAlī ibn Muḥammadal-Bustī (d. 401 AH). Well-known poet and *ḥadīth* specialist who hailed from the town of Bust near Sijistān in Central Asia.

02 Ismāʿīl ibn al-Muqrī (d. 1434) North Yemeni scholar, Shāfiʿī jurist, and poet, author of famous works of Shāfiʿī jurisprudence. He died and was buried in Zabīd.

03 Qārūn, the Biblical Qorah, is an Israelite who lived in Egypt in the days of Moses—may peace be upon him—and was so rich that it took several men to carry the keys to his treasures.

of the worlds.[68] None are granted it save those who are patient, and none is granted it save one who is fortunate indeed.[69]

38

STRUCTURING TIME

The Proof of Islam—may God's mercy be on him—writes in his book *The Beginning of Guidance* [*Bidāyat al-Hidāya*], in the chapter on 'Preparing for the Ritual Prayers',

You should not neglect your time or use it haphazardly; on the contrary you should bring yourself to account, structure your *awrād* and other practices during each day and night, and assign to each period a fixed and specific function. This is how to bring out the *baraka* in each period. But if you leave yourself adrift, aimlessly wandering as cattle do, not knowing how to occupy yourself at every moment, your time will be lost. It is nothing other than your life, and your life is the capital that you make use of to reach perpetual felicity in the proximity of God the Exalted. Each of your breaths is a priceless jewel, since each of them is irreplaceable and, once gone, can never be retrieved. Do not be like the deceived fools who are joyous because each day their wealth increases while their life shortens. What good is an increase in wealth when life grows ever shorter? Therefore, be joyous only for an increase in knowledge or in good works, for they are your two companions who will accompany you in your grave when your family, wealth, children and friends stay behind.

Then he writes-may God's mercy be on him—'Know that a night and a day comprise twenty-four hours; therefore, do not sleep more than eight hours, for it should suffice you to realize that if you were to live, say sixty years, you would have wasted twenty, which is one third.'

And he says—may God's mercy be on him—'If you do this (that is, remember death, prepare for its coming, and patiently obey God the Exalted), you will know endless joy when death arrives. Whereas if you are complacent and procrastinate, death will come to you at an unforeseen moment and you will know regrets without end. At dawn people are grateful for the distance they covered during the night. With death certainty comes to you; you will surely have its experience, in time.'

Knowledge of the contents of this [aforementioned] small book is sufficient to obviate the need for the intelligent, alert believer, who is active in worship, to seek lengthier treatises dealing with the same matters. A Shādhilī scholar once said, 'What Imām al-Ghazālī ﵁ has included in the *Beginning* is sufficient for a Sufi beginner; what he has included in *The Way of the Worshippers* [*Minhāj al-ʿĀbidīn*] suffices the one in the middle; and the *Revival of the Religious Sciences* [*Iḥyā' ʿUlūm al-Dīn*] is enough for the one near the end of the path.' The matter is evidently so for whoever is fair in his judgment and aims to adorn himself with the best of virtues and attributes. God grants success, there is no other Lord.

How excellent are the poet's words,

Gather provision for the inescapable;
Mankind's appointment is the Resurrection.
Will it please you to be with those whose
Provision is abundant while yours is amiss?

Also, the famous poem which begins with,

I see that daylight illumines for you
The upright road from which you swerve.

And where he says,

I shall advise at times, and at times counsel;
Perhaps that will avail, perhaps this.
If you prefer this world over the Next
For its attractions, an evil choice it is.
When aim and purpose are
Who are the best of us, who the worst?
We are prey to the illusion of the green branches
Of hope which never bear fruit.

This is a blessed poem belonging to a certain man from Yemen. Our master the Quṭb Shaykh ʿUmar al-Miḥdār ibn ʿAbd al-Raḥmān[01] used to like it and so did the Shaykh, the exemplar Fadl ibn ʿAbdallāh al-Tarīmī

01 ʿUmar son of Imām ʿAbd al-Raḥmān al-Saqqāf Bā-ʿAlawī, known as al-Miḥdār (d.

al-Shiḥrī[01]—may God have mercy on them and spread their benefit and that of all His virtuous servants.

833 AH). Supreme ʿAlawī scholar and saint of his day who lived and died in Tarīm and whose tomb is in the Zanbal portion of the Bashshār Cemetery.

01 Fadl ibn ʿAbdallāh. Eleventh century AH scholar, Sufi, and high-ranking saint from the coastal town of al-Shiḥr in Southern Yemen.

39

ʿALĪ AND THE WORLD

It has been related that when Muʿāwiya[01] asked Ḍirār ibn Ḍamra to describe ʿAlī to him, the latter said, 'Exempt me, O Commander of the Faithful!' But he said, 'I shall not!' at which he said, 'Then I will say this: He was, may God be pleased with him, far-sighted and of mighty strength. His words were decisive, his judgment just. He liked coarse food and short clothes, felt estranged from the world and its attractions, but at ease with night, its darkness and loneliness. I bear witness that I saw him once when night had fallen and the stars had risen, wakeful in his retreat, clutching his beard, restless as though wounded, weeping sorrowfully, saying, 'O world! Deceive other than I! Is it for me that you beautify yourself? Is it to me that you show yourself? I have divorced you thrice, there can be no return, for your span is short, your worth insignificant, and your danger great! Ah! The scarcity of provision, the length of the way, and the estrangement of travelling!' Muʿāwiya wept, raising his sleeve to his face to stem his tears as best as he could, and then said, 'May God have mercy on Abu'l-Ḥasan! He was, by God, truly as you say!'

There is evidence to indicate that Muʿāwiya regretted opposing and warring with ʿAlī, as others too regretted it, like ʿĀisha, Ṭalḥa[02], and al-Zubayr[03]—may God be pleased with them. ʿAbdallāh ibn ʿUmar—may God be pleased with both—regretted his abstention from fighting alongside ʿAlī

01 Muʿāwiya ibn Abī Sufyān (d. 60 AH). Qurayshi Companion of the Prophet—may God's blessings and peace be upon him and his family—and first Umayyad Caliph.

02 Ṭalḥa ibn ʿUbayd-Allāh (d. 36 AH aged 64) important early Companion from the clan of Tūym, Abū Bakr's clan, and one of the Ten promised Paradise.

03 Al-Zubayr ibn al-ʿAwwām (d. 36 AH). A paternal cousin of the Prophet—may God's blessings and peace be upon him and his family—who accepted Islam very early in Mecca at a young age. He was an intrepid warrior and one of the ten Companions promised Paradise.

🕮 but the command of God was a destiny decreed.⁷⁰ May God be pleased with all the Companions of the Messenger of God.

How good is the saying of the author of the *Burda*⁰¹, in exhortation to gather provision for the Hereafter,

> *I beg of God forgiveness for saying and not doing,*
> *Thus attributing offspring to one sterile.*
> *I ordered you to do good but myself did not obey;*
> *Neither was I upright; how can I ask you to be?*
> *I stored no provisions of devotions before death,*
> *I prayed and fasted only when obliged.⁰²*
> *I neglected the example of he who kept awake*
> *In the dark so long that his feet suffered and were swollen⁰³*
> *Who braced his stomach from hunger*
> *Tying stones to his gracious side.*
> *Proud mountains of gold offered themselves*
> *To him who showed them how pride should be.⁰⁴*
> *His detachment was emphasized by his want*
> *But want cannot overcome Divine protection.⁰⁵*
> *How can want attract to the world he*
> *Without whom the world would not exist.*

---

01   The *Burda* (the Mantle) is the most famous poem in praise of the Prophet — may God's blessings and peace be upon him and his family — Its author is Imam al-Būṣīrī, a disciple of the famous Shaykh Abu'l-'Abbās al-Mursī. He was buried in Alexandria, in a mosque next to that of his Shaykh, by the side of the sea.

02   The author accuses himself of restricting himself to the obligatory acts of worship, knowing full well that the *Sunna* involves a multitude of supererogatory practices.

03   The Prophet — may God's blessings and peace be upon him and his family — stood so long in prayer at night that his feet became swollen. Noticing this, the Lady 'Aisha asked him, 'Why do you do this when God has forgiven you everything past and to come?' to which he simply answered: 'Should I not be a thankful servant?' [Bukhārī, *Ṣaḥīḥ*, 4837]

04   God offered to the Prophet — may God's blessings and peace be upon him and his family — to turn the valley of Mecca into gold for him. He refused, preferring to remain poor so that he would *'eat one day and be grateful, then sleep hungry another day and be patient.'* [Tirmidhī, *Sunan*, 2347]

05   Divine protection to Prophets gives them infallibility, the erasure of the possibility of surrendering to temptation.

Muḥammad, master of the two worlds and the two weighty beings,
And the two groups, the Arabs and the non-Arabs.[01]

He also says in his poem in Lām,

Till when shall you remain absorbed in your pleasures
When you shall account for every act?
Every day you leave repentance for the morrow,
The power of your resolution dissolved by delay.

And al-Khalīl ibn Aḥmad[02] says—may God's mercy be on him—

It is but one night after the other,
Day after day and month after month.
Stages drawing new things to decay
And lowering the remains of noblemen into the grave.
They give the wives of jealous men to others
And take that which the avaricious had set by.

Another poet says,

Wealth I see adds to your longing
For the world as if you are to live forever.
Is there a limit that you might reach,
Where you would say: enough! I am satisfied!

---

01 ʿAjam: 'non-Arabs'. This word was originally used to denote an inability to express oneself, either totally or partially. The Arabs were proud of their eloquence, being a desert people with an auditory culture who could memorize poems hundreds of verses long after one hearing. To them everyone else was ʿAjamī, ineloquent. This referred primarily to the Persians, then by extension to all non-Arabs.

02 Al-Khalīl ibn Aḥmad al-Farāhīdī (d. 170 AH). One of the principal founders of Arabic philology and undisputed founder of the science of metrics. He lived a very poor life in Basra where he died.

40

THE COMPANIONS AND THE WORLD

It is related that when he breathed, Abū Bakr al-Ṣiddīq[01]—may God be pleased with him—exhaled the smell of grilled liver.[02] It was later said that this was because of his excessive fear of God the Exalted, because of his grief and sorrow at the death of the Messenger of God—may blessings and peace be upon him and his family—or due to the [effects of] viper's venom, for he had been bitten while blocking a hole with his heel to protect the Messenger of God—may blessings and peace be upon him—on the night they were in the cave,[03] or lastly because of poisoned food he once ate together with a Bedouin whose name was, I think, al-Ḥārith. This man had knowledge of medicine, and when he tasted the poison told Abū Bakr, 'The food is poisoned, a year from now we shall both die from it.' It is said that they both did die on the same day.

When Abū Bakr fell ill they asked him if they should not bring him a physician, but he answered, 'The Physician has looked at me and said, "I do as I will".' Or according to another version, 'It is the Physician who has made me ill,' meaning by that the Lord—Exalted is He. When he felt weak and designated ʿUmar as his successor, he ordered them to return the

---

01 Abū Bakr al-Ṣiddīq, (d. 13 AH) the closest companion, first successor, and father-in-law of the Prophet—may God's blessings and peace be upon him and his family.

02 This is an example of how, for some people, certain things from the subtle 'World of Similitudes' are perceived by the physical senses. It was certainly not a purely physical phenomenon, nor was it a purely subtle one, but something spanning the two domains.

03 The cave of *Thawr*, on top of a small mountain south of Mecca. This is where the Blessed Prophet and Abū Bakr hid from the disbelievers after the Blessed Prophet had decided to emigrate to Madina.

little that had been his share from the treasury to 'Umar, at which the latter remarked, 'He has made it hard for those who will succeed him.'

As for 'Umar ibn al-Khaṭṭāb—may God the Exalted be pleased with him-he ate barley during his caliphate and patched his own clothes. His conduct is very well known. He would read verses from the Book of God during his night prayers, then become overwhelmed with fear, fall to the ground, become ill, stay at home, and people would visit him the same way they visited the sick.

As for 'Uthmān ibn 'Affān[01]—may God be pleased with him—he used to give the Caliph's food to the people, then enter his house and eat bread dipped in oil. When the perpetrators of outrage climbed onto his house, entered it and murdered him, he said, 'O God! Unite the Nation of Muḥammad!' The Qur'ān was on his lap and some of his blood fell on His words—Exalted is He—**God will suffice you against them, and He is the Hearing, the Knowing.**[71] Later on, one of the Companions, possibly 'Abdallāh ibn Salām[02], said, 'Had he not prayed that God the Exalted should unite the Nation, it would never have united after him.'

As for 'Alī ibn Abī Ṭālib—may God be pleased with him—he used to eat barley as a Caliph and to shorten the sleeves of his shirts to the wrist or the fingertips. When criticized for the roughness of his lifestyle and clothes, he replied—may God be pleased with him—'It is so that the Muslims may take me as example and not despise the poor because of their poverty.'

This was the pattern of behavior of the first among the Emigrants and Helpers—may God be pleased with them all. They took little from this world and confined themselves to essentials, the strictly necessary. Their biographies testify to this, those of such people as 'Ammār[03], Abū 'Ubayda

---

01 'Uthmān ibn 'Affān (d. 35 AH). Eminent Companion who was given two of the Prophet' daughters to marry in succession before becoming the third Caliph of Islam.

02 'Abdallāh ibn Salām (d. 43 AH) A Companion of the Prophet—may God's blessings and peace be upon him and his family. He was said to be a descendent of the Prophet Joseph—may peace be upon him—and before accepting Islam was one of the Jewish rabbis of Madina. He was known among the Companions to be one of the people of the Garden because he had once had a dream vision and had narrated it to the Prophet—may God's blessings and peace be upon him and his family—who told him it meant he was sure to hold fast to Islam until the end of his life and was thus destined for the Garden. [Bukhārī, *Ṣaḥīḥ*, 3813]

03 'Ammār ibn Yāsir (d. 37 AH). An early Muslim, who was tortured in Mecca, together

ibn al-Jarrāḥ[01], Muʿādh ibn Jabal[02], Abū Dharr[03], Ḥudhayfa[04], Khabbāb ibn al-Aratt[05] and ʿItbān ibn Mālik[06]. Thus, also were the leaders among the Followers, such as Imām ʿAlī Zayn al-ʿAbidīn, son of Imām Ḥusayn, his son al-Bāqir, his grandson Jaʿfar, Saʿīd ibn al-Musayyab[07], ʿUmar ibn

---

with his two parents, for their faith. He lost an ear to the Najdi Bedouins at the Battle of Yamāma during the Wars of apostasy and was martyred fighting in Battle of Siffin.

01 Abū ʿUbayda ibn al-Jarrāḥ (d. 18 AH). One of the very early Companions, given by the Prophet—may God's blessings and peace be upon him and his family—the title of "Trustee of this Nation" and one of the Ten who were solemnly promised Paradise. A very gentle and soft-hearted man, he was nevertheless a great warrior and went on to become one of the greatest generals of the generation of the Companions.

02 Muʿādh ibn Jabal (d. 18 AH). Anṣārī Companion of the Prophet—may God's blessings and peace be upon him and his family—who declared him to be the Leader of the Scholars on Judgment Day and sent him as governor to the Yemen.

03 Abū Dharr al-Ghifārī (d. 32 AH) Eminent Companion and one of *Ahl al-Ṣuffa* or People of the Shelter, the poor Emigrants who slept under a shelter at the back of the Prophet's Mosque. As were most members of this group, he was a noted ascetic, later to become a leading narrator of ḥadīth.

04 Ḥudhayfa ibn al-Yamān (d. 36 AH). One of the great Companions who was entrusted by the Prophet—may God's blessings and peace be upon him and his family—with knowledge of the hypocrites in Madina, so that he knew who was one them and who was not, but would not reveal this to anyone. Narrator of many ḥadīths concerning the trials and seditions of the end of time.

05 Khabbāb ibn al-Araṭṭ (d. 37 AH). One of the earliest Muslims in Mecca, he suffered severe persecution and torture to renounce his religion. He died on the outskirts of Kūfa upon his return from the Battle of Ṣiffīn and his Funeral Prayer was led by Imām ʿAlī.

06 ʿItbān ibn Mālik (Exact date of death unknown). Companion of the Prophet—may God's blessings and peace be upon him and his family—and leader of the Banī Sālim ibn ʿAwf branch of the Madinan tribe of Khazraj.

07 Saʿīd ibn al-Musayyab (d. 93). One of the most eminent if not the most eminent of all Tābiʿīn or Followers of the Companions in Madina.

ʿAbd al-ʿAzīz[01], Uways al-Qarnī[02], Harim ibn Ḥayyān[03], al-Ḥasan al-Baṣrī[04], Abū Ḥāzim al-Madanī[05], and ʿAṭā' ibn al-Sā'ib[06]. So too were the Followers of the Followers, such as the four Imāms, Fuḍayl ibn ʿIyāḍ, Ibrāhīm ibn Adham, Ibrāhīm al-Taymī[07], Mālik ibn Dīnār[08], and others of the first three

---

01 ʿUmar ibn ʿAbd al-Azīz (d. 101 AH). Righteous Umayyad Caliph. He put an end to the vilification of Imām ʿAlī in the mosques of the Umayyad Empire and in his short reign *Zakāt* was so justly gathered and distributed that poverty all but disappeared.

02 Uways al-Qarnī (d. c. 37 AH). A Yemeni man of God who was prevented by his mother's illness from joining the Prophet—may God's blessings and peace be upon him and his family—in Madina. He was able to travel only after his mother had died, by which time the Prophet—may God's blessings and peace be upon him and his family—had also died but had told ʿUmar and ʿAlī to seek him among the pilgrims of the Yemen and when they found him ask him for his prayers. These were unusual instructions, for ʿUmar and ʿAlī were among the very greatest Companions and thus supremely high ranking in the hierarchy of sainthood and to ask them to go searching for an obscure Yemeni who had never met the Prophet—may God's blessings and peace be upon him and his family—and ask him to pray for them rather than they for him was puzzling to say the least. Clearly the Prophet—may God's blessings and peace be upon him and his family—wished to make it known that there were such people in his Community, obscure yet high ranking, whose prayers deserved to be sought.

03 Harim ibn Ḥayyān. A Follower who worked for ʿUmar ibn al-Khaṭṭāb. He went searching for Uways al-Qarnī wishing to benefit from him spiritually, found him on the banks of the Tigris and after some beautiful spiritual exchanges was asked by him never to try to see him again.

04 See footnote 20.

05 Abū Ḥāzim al-Madanī (d. 140 or 144 AH). Follower who lived in Madina and received and transmitted *ḥadīth* from the Companions.

06 ʿAṭā ibn al-Sāib (d. 136 AH) Follower of the Followers, studied under the great Follower Saʿīd ibn Jubayr and transmitted *ḥadīth* from his own father and al-Ḥasan al-Baṣrī. Among those who took from him were illustrious scholars such as Imām Abū Ḥanīfa, Sufyān al-Thawrī and Sufyān ibn ʿUyayna.

07 Ibrāhīm al-Taymī (d. c. 93 AH). A scholar, ascetic, and *ḥadīth* narrator of Kūfa. The story of his death is that he was once with a group of people when the bloodthirsty governor of Iraq al-Ḥajjāj ibn Yūsuf asked them about Ibrāhīm al-Nakhaʿī whom he wished to arrest. When he asked, "Where is Ibrāhīm?" he stepped forward saying, "I am Ibrāhīm." He was arrested and jailed in his stead and died of maltreatment in prison.

08 Mālik ibn Dīnār (d. between 123 and 131 AH). Tābiʿī or Follower who transmitted *ḥadīth* from Anas ibn Mālik. He lived and died in Basra, earned his living by writing Qur'āns, and was known for his asceticism.

best generations. He said—may blessings and peace be upon him—*The best generation is my generation, then those who will follow them, them those who will follow them,'* repeating *['then those who will follow them']* two or three times.[72] And he said—may blessings and peace be upon him—*In each of my community's generations there will be outstrippers.*[01] The matter is indeed so; but they are growing smaller in number, and at certain periods conceal themselves, but are never altogether absent. He said—may peace be upon him—*A community will never perish which has me at its beginning and Jesus the son of Mary at its end.*[73] We have mentioned some glimpses of the ways of our Predecessors in our book *The Complete Summons* [*al-Daʿwa al-Tāmma*][02], and made frequent references to them in our poem which begins with,

O you who ask about my tears and the sighs shaking my ribs

An ample commentary on this poem was made by one of our closest companions, the *sayyid*, the scholar, the authority, the Sufi, the *Sharīf* Aḥmad ibn Zayn al-Ḥabashī ʿAlawī[03]. He mentions some of the merits of every person mentioned in the poem. As for this [present] book, because our aim is to make it brief, we have refrained from elaborating on their merits. They are mentioned in abundance in other works such as *Siyar al-Salaf,*[04] *Majmaʿ al-Aḥbāb,*[05] Qūt al-Qulūb by Imām Abū Ṭālib al-Makkī[06], and the *Iḥyā'* of the Proof of Islam, as well as other works of biography and history.

---

01 Abū Nuʿaym, *Ḥilyat al-Awliyā*, 1:8. The Outstrippers are none other than the Foremost, *al-Sābiqūn*, referred to in the following Qur'ānic passage: **and the Foremost, the Foremost, those are the ones brought nigh, in the Gardens of Delight; a multitude of the ancients and a few of the later folk.** [Qur'ān, 56:10–14]

02 Imām ʿAbdallāh al-Ḥaddād, *The Complete Summons and General Reminder*, Fons Vitae, Louisville, 2016.

03 Aḥmad ibn Zayn al-Ḥabashī Bā-ʿAlawī (d. 1145 AH) Authoritative scholar, jurist and author of Ḥaḍramawt and close disciple and friend of Imām al-Ḥaddād.

04 *Siyar al-Salaf al-Ṣāliḥīn* (*Biographies of the Virtuous predecessors*) by Ismāʿīl ibn Muḥammad al-Aṣbahānī (d. 535 AH) is a compilation of biographies of the Companions and Followers. The author is a scholar of *Tafsīr, Ḥadīth, and Fiqh*, of Qurayshi ancestry.

05 *Majmaʿ al-Aḥbāb, Gathering of the Loved Ones*, is a summary of Abū Nuʿaym's famous *Ḥilyat al-Awliyā* authored by Muḥammad ibn al-Ḥasan al-Wāsitī (d. 776 AH).

06 *Qūt al-Qulūb* (*Sustenance for the Hearts*) by Abū Ṭālib al-Makkī (d. 386 AH) the famous and influential precursor of the *Revival of Religious Sciences* of Ghazālī. The author was a Mālikī jurist and Sufi who spent the last years of his life in Mecca and was buried there.

Let him who wishes to know the pattern of our Virtuous Predecessors, the Companions, Followers and Followers of the Followers, peruse them. He will then know how they gave precedence to the life-to-come over this one, were content with little of this world, were neither deceived by this world's beauty, nor eager to enjoy its pleasures, even though they were fully able to do so in a lawful manner.

Conclusion

These [following] are verses from the Book of God—August and Majestic—traditions from the *Sunna* of the Messenger of God—may God's blessings be upon him and his family—and sayings of the Virtuous Predecessors who guided to the Path of God—may God spread their benefit.

God—High and Majestic—says, **And guard yourselves against a day in which you will be brought back to God, then every soul will be paid in full that which it had earned, and they will not be wronged.**[74] It is on record that this was the last verse of the Qur'ān to be revealed, and that the Messenger of God—may blessings and peace be upon him—lived only ten days thereafter.

God—Exalted is He—says, **O you who believe! Have fortitude, endurance, vigilance, and *taqwā*, that you may succeed.**[75] He—Exalted is He—also says **O you who believe! Obey God, and obey the Messenger and those of you who are in authority, and if you have a dispute concerning any matter, refer it to God and the Messenger, if you are believers in God and the Last Day. This is better and of fairer consequence.**[76] He—Exalted is He—also says **There is no blame on those who believe and do good for what they may have eaten, if they have *taqwā*, believe, and do good works, then have *taqwā* and believe, then have *taqwā* and act with excellence; and God loves those who act with excellence.**[77] He—Exalted is He—also says **Hold to forgiveness, enjoin kindness, and turn away from the ignorant.**[78] He—Exalted is He—also says **And you are not occupied with any matter, and you recite not of the Qur'ān, and you perform no act, but that We are Witnessing what you engage yourselves in. And not an atom's weight that is in the earth or in the sky escapes your Lord, nor what is less than that or greater, but it is in a Clear Book.**[79] He—Exalted is He—also says **Those who desire the life of the world and its pomp, We shall repay them their deeds in it, and in it**

they will not be wronged.[80] He—Exalted is He—also says **I do not exculpate myself, indeed the soul incites to evil, save where my Lord has mercy; verily my Lord is indeed Forgiving, Compassionate.**[81] He—Exalted is He—also says **Strain not your eyes toward that which We cause some pairs among them to enjoy, and be not grieved on their account, and lower your wing to the believers.**[82] He—Exalted is He—also says **God is indeed with those who have *taqwā* and those who act excellently.**[83] He—Exalted is He—also says **Whoever hopes for the meeting with his Lord, let him do good works and associate no one with his Lord in worship.**[84] He—Exalted is He—also says **And enjoin upon your family worship, and be constant therein. We ask you for no provision, We provide for you; and the sequel is for *taqwā*.**[85] He—Exalted is He—also says **Did you think that We created you for nothing, and that to Us you shall not be returned?**[86] He—Exalted is He—also says **Those who strive in Us, We shall surely guide them to Our paths, indeed God is with those who act excellently.**[87] He—Exalted is He—also says **We offered the Trust to the heavens, the earth, and the mountains, and they refused to bear it and shrank from it; but man assumed it. Assuredly, he is ever unjust and ignorant.**[88] He—Exalted is He—also says **They esteemed not God as is His right; and the whole earth is His handful on the Day of Rising, and the heavens shall be rolled in His Right Hand. Transcendent is He and Exalted above that which they partner.**[89] He—Exalted is He—also says **Or do those who work ill deeds suppose that We shall make them as those who believe and do good works, equal in life and death? Evil indeed is their judgment!**[90] He—Exalted is He—also says **O you who believe! Fear God; and let each soul look to what it sends ahead for the morrow. Fear God; He is indeed Aware of what you do.**[91] He—Exalted is He—also says **O you who believe! Turn unto God in a repentance sincere, that your Lord remit your sins and make you enter Gardens underneath which rivers flow. On the Day when God will not let down the Prophet and those who believe with him: their light will run before them and on their right hands, and they will say: Our Lord! Complete our light for us, and forgive us, You are Able to do all things.**[92]

The Messenger of God ﷺ said, *O people! Repent unto God before you die! Hasten to good works before you become too occupied, and strengthen that which is between you and your Lord by remembering Him in abundance.*[93] He ﷺ also said *Hasten to act; there will come temptations like patches of dark night; then a man will wake up a believer and by nightfall become a disbeliever, or be a believer in the evening and become a disbeliever by morning, and he will sell his religion for a little of what the world has to offer.*[94] He ﷺ also said *Those who fear set out at nightfall; and those who set out at nightfall reach their destination. Verily the merchandise of God is precious! Verily the merchandise of God is the Garden!*[95] He ﷺ also said *The head of [all] wisdom is the fear of God.*[96] He ﷺ also said *It is part of being a good Muslim for a man to leave that which does not concern him.*[97] He ﷺ also said *Leave that which arouses your doubt for that which does not.*[98] He ﷺ also said *None of you is a believer until he wishes for his brother what he wishes for himself.*[99] He ﷺ also said *One of the things which have come down to mankind from the sayings of ancient Prophethood is: "If you have no shame, do what you will!"*[100] He ﷺ also said *God has imposed obligations; therefore do not allow them to be wasted! He has established prohibitions; so do not violate them! He has drawn limits; therefore do not transgress them! And He has kept silent about certain things out of compassion for you, not out of forgetfulness; so do not search for them!'*[101] He ﷺ also said *Whoever sees a reprehensible thing let him change it with his hand. If he cannot, then with his tongue. If he cannot do that, then with his heart; and that is the weakest [degree] of faith.*[102] He ﷺ also said *None of you is a believer until his desire conforms to what I have brought.*[103] He ﷺ also said *Faith has seventy-odd branches, the highest of which is to say Lā ilāha illa'Llāh, and the lowest to remove a harmful thing from the road.*[104] He ﷺ also said *I have seen nothing like a Garden whose seeker sleeps, or a Fire whose evader sleeps.*[105] He ﷺ also said *The Garden is surrounded with hateful things, and the Fire with pleasures.*[106] He ﷺ also said *Never does the son of Adam fill a worse vessel than his stomach. A few morsels to keep his back straight should suffice the son of Adam. But if he must, then let him give one third to his food, one third to his beverage, and one third to his breath.*[107] Another tradition instructs the Muslims to eat only half their stomach fill, and accustom their bodies to it, for this is one part of Prophethood.[108] He ﷺ also said *Three things save and three ruin. As for the saving things, they are to fear God secretly and in public, to speak the truth whether pleased or angry, and to be moderate in both affluence and poverty. As for the ruinous things, they are passion that one follows, greed that one obeys, and the admiration of a man for himself.*[109] He ﷺ also said *Seven will be shaded by God under His shade on the day when there will be no shade but His: a just leader; a young man who grew up in the worship of God—August and Majestic is He; a man whose heart remains attached to the mosque; two men who loved each other for God the Exalted, meeting thus and separating thus; a man who was invited by a woman of rank and beauty but who said, 'I fear God!'; a man who gave alms and concealed them so that his left hand did not know what his right hand had spent; and a man who remembered God when alone and whose eyes overflowed [with tears.]*[110] He ﷺ also said *It is as if death had been decreed [only] on others, as if truth was an obligation only on others, as if the dead that we escort [to their graves] are on a journey from which they will soon return to us: we lay them in their graves, then spend what they have left behind as if we were to live eternally after them, forgetting all advice and feeling secure from all disaster.*[111] He ﷺ also said *I have left two counselors among you, one that speaks and another that is silent; the one that speaks is the Book of God, and the one that is silent is Death.*[112] He ﷺ also said *The feet of a servant will not move on Judgment Day until he has been questioned about five things: his lifetime and how he exhausted it; his youth and how it was worn out; his wealth, and wherefrom he obtained it and how he spent it; and his knowledge, and what he did with it.*[113]

Prophet ﷺ said *There are nine things which, when they occur among the people, will be accompanied by nine other things:*

When adultery becomes rife, sudden death becomes rife.

When they withhold Zakāt, God will withhold the rains.

When they cheat in their weights, they will be stricken with famine.

When they judge unjustly, injustice and aggression will spread among them.

When they break their pledges, God will let their enemy prevail over them.

When they abandon exhorting to good, their affairs will become disturbed.

When they abandon forbidding evil, the worst among them will become their rulers.

When they neglect their kinship ties, their wealth will be given to the worst among them.

When they commit sins, they will be stricken with afflictions.[01]

---

01 This is not a single *ḥadīth*, but to convey the intended meaning in a single passage the Imām has here quoted portions from several *hadīths* such as among others the following: *O Emigrants, five things, if you become afflicted with them—and I ask God to protect you from witnessing them: Indecency never becomes rife among a people and they make it public without their suffering from plagues and illnesses that had not previously existed in their ancestors. Neither will they cheat in weights and measures, without being seized with famines and oppression from the ruler. Nor will they withhold the Zakāt of their money without the sky withholding its rain; were it not for the animals they would*

ʿAlī—may God honor his countenance—said, 'Were the veil to be removed I would not increase in certitude.' And, 'Suppose that God were to forgive those who did wrong, would they not still have missed the rewards of those who did good?' And he said—may God be pleased with him—'Blessed are those who renounce the world and wish for the Hereafter. They are those who use the earth as a rug, its dust as a bed, its water as perfume, and make prayers and the Qur'ān their robes; thus they reject the world according to the pattern of Jesus ﷺ.'

ʿAlī Zayn al-ʿAbidīn, son of al-Ḥusayn—may God be pleased with them—said, 'God has concealed three within three. He has concealed His good-pleasure in His obedience; therefore, despise no act of obedience lest His good pleasure be within it. And He has concealed His abhorrence in rebellion; therefore, underestimate no act of rebellion, lest His abhorrence be therein. And He has concealed His Friends in His creation; therefore, despise none of His creatures, for he may be a Friend of God.' And he said, 'The weapon of the wicked is corrupt speech.'

His son Muḥammad al-Bāqir said, 'I had a companion who was, in my eyes, very great. What made him great in my eyes was the insignificance of the world in his.'

His son Jaʿfar al-Sādiq said, 'Safety has become so rare that the way to it has become hidden; if it is in anything at all it will be in anonymity. If it is not in anonymity, it will be in divestment; if it is not in divestment, it will be in silence, which is not like divestment. If it is not in silence, it will be in the words of the Righteous Predecessors. Fortunate is he who finds himself free from preoccupation.'

---

have no rain at all. Nor will they break God's pledge and that of His Messenger without the enemy being given the upper hand against them and seizing some of their possessions. So long as their leaders do not rule by the Book of God, nor conform to what God has sent down, He will cause their aggression to be among one another. [Ibn Māja, *Sunan,* 4019] *When my community commits fifteen things it will become afflicted.* "What are they, O Messenger of God?" They asked. He answered, *When revenues become an exclusive prerogative, trust is treated as booty, zakāt is considered a burden, men obey their wives and are disloyal to their mothers, draw their friends nearer, while pushing their fathers away, voices are raised in the mosques, the vilest among a people becomes their chief, a man is honored for fear of his evil, alcohol is drunk, silk is worn, girl singers and concerts become habitual, and the last of this community curse the first, let them expect violent storms, or sinking into the ground, or mutations.* [Tirmidhī, *Sunan,* 2210, 2211]

Al-Ḥasan al-Baṣrī ﷺ said, 'Death has exposed the world and left no joy in it for any intelligent person.' And: 'Beware of hoping for forgiveness without working for it. Some people have continued to be deceived by such hopes until they departed from the world bankrupt.' And, 'Beware of these hopes, they are the valleys of the fools.'

ʿUmar ibn ʿAbd al-ʿAzīz ﷺ once received a garment costing one thousand dirhams and remarked, 'How beautiful it is; were it not for some roughness in it!' But after he became Caliph they would bring him a garment costing ten dirhams and he would say, 'How beautiful it is; were it not for some softness in it.' He was the one—may God be pleased with him—who forbade them to curse the Commander of the Faithful, ʿAlī ibn Abī Ṭālib—may God honor his countenance—on the pulpits and to replace the curses with, **Our Lord, Forgive us and our brethren who preceded us in the faith,** to the end of the verse[114]; or, **God enjoins justice and excellence,** to the end of the verse.[115]

How admirable is the saying of *al-Sharīf* al-Raḍī[01] in addressing ʿUmar ibn ʿAbd al-ʿAzīz,

Son of ʿAbd al-ʿAzīz! Were the eyes to weep
For an Umayyad I would weep for you.
You rescued us from insult and slander;
If reward were possible I would repay you.

Abū Ḥāzim al-Madanī—may God have mercy on him—said, 'That which has gone by of the world is a dream, while that which remains is [no more than] hopes.' And, 'You never extend your hand toward anything of the world without finding that some corrupt person has preceded you to it.'

When Mālik ibn Dīnār—may God have mercy on him—went out of his house, he pulled the door closed with a piece of rope, saying, 'Were it not for the dogs I would leave it open.' This was because it was empty of worldly things. A woman once stole his Qur'ān and his blanket. He followed her calling, 'You there! Do you have a son who can read? Do you have a husband who can read?' She answered, 'No!' So he said, 'Give me back the Qur'ān and keep the blanket.'

Al-Fuḍayl ibn ʿIyāḍ ﷺ said, 'To abandon action because of other people

---

01 *Al-Sharīf* al-Raḍī is a descendent of Imām Mūsā son of Jaʿfar al-Ṣādiq and was one of the greatest poets of Baghdad (d. 406 AH)

is ostentation; to act because of them is idolatry; and sincerity is that God should save you from both.' And, 'Had the world been perishable gold and the life-to-come permanent clay, we should still prefer permanent clay to perishable gold. What then when the life-to-come is permanent gold and the world perishable clay?'

Ibrāhīm ibn Adham ﷺ said, 'I once passed by a stone which bore the following legend, "Turn me over and learn a lesson". I turned it over and found these words, "You do not practice what you know, so how can you ask for the knowledge of that which you do not know?"' It was once said to him, 'Meat has become expensive!' He replied, 'Cheapen it by abandoning it!' And he said, 'Make your food pure and it will do you no harm to not keep vigil at night and not fast by day.'[01]

A man once said to Dāwūd al-Ṭā'ī[02] ﷺ 'Counsel me!' He said, 'Fast from the world, break your fast with the life-to-come, and flee from people as you would flee from a lion.'

Maʿrūf al-Karkhī[03] ﷺ once said, 'I once passed by Ibn al-Sammāk[04] as he was counseling the people and heard him say, "The one who approaches God, God approaches him; the one who turns away from God, God turns away from him; and as for the man who does one time this and one time that, God treats him likewise." I told my master ʿAlī ibn Mūsā al-Riḍā[05] about this, and he said, "What you have heard should suffice you as counsel." So I left everything [of the world's preoccupations] except the service of my master ʿAlī ibn Mūsā al-Riḍā—may God be pleased with him.'

---

01 The intention is not that one should abandon these practices, but rather that while they are required, they are useless without maintaining a *ḥalāl* and moderate diet.

02 Dāwūd al-Ṭāī (d. 165 AH). Famous Sufi of Baghdad who started by being a student of Imām Abū Ḥanīfa, then having mastered the religious sciences turned to ascetic practices.

03 Maʿrūf al-Karkhī (d. 200 AH). Major early Sufi who lived and died in Baghdad in the area called al-Karkh, by the Tigris River. He accepted Islam at the hands of Imām ʿAlī son of Imām Mūsā al-Kāẓim and where he was the disciple of Dāwūd al-Ṭāī, the teacher of Sarī al-Saqaṭī and a major link in the main Sufi chain.

04 Ibn al-Sammāk (d. 183 AH) Scholar, preacher of renown and transmitter of *ḥadīth* from Kūfa who came to Baghdad during the days of the Abbasid Caliph Hārūn al-Rashīd.

05 Imām ʿAlī Riẓā son of Mūsā al-Kāẓim son of Jaʿfar al-Ṣādiq (d. 203 AH) Great scholar, saint, and transmitter of *ḥadīth*, considered by the Twelver Shīʿa to be their eighth Imām.

Sarī al-Saqaṭī[01] ﵀ said, 'Alive is he who knows God the Exalted; astray is he who loves the world. The intelligent watch themselves and the fools come and go in vacuous activities.'

Al-Junayd[02] ﵀ once said, 'We did not take Sufism from words and sayings but from hunger, night vigils, leaving the world, and abstaining from familiar and likeable things.' When he was about to die he was heard completing a recitation of the Qur'ān and starting a new one from the beginning. They asked him, 'In this state of yours?' He replied, 'Yes! And who is more in need than I when my scroll is being folded up?'

Bishr al-Ḥāfī said:

He who honors the world is abased And on Judgment Day dishonored
But he who disdains it today That day will find incomparable honor

He was once seen thinly dressed on an extremely cold day. When questioned about this he replied, 'I remembered the poor in this cold, and how they are suffering. I have nothing to comfort them with, so I comfort them with myself.'

Al-Ḥārith al-Muḥāsibī[03] said, 'The one who adorns his inward with vigilance and sincerity, God adorns his outward with striving and following the *Sunna*.'

Yaḥyā ibn Muʿādh[04] said, 'I left the world because of its excessive toil, the swiftness with which it perishes, the scarcity of its wealth, and the villainy of its partners.'

Sahl al-Tustarī[05] said, 'There is no helper save God, no guide save the Messenger of God, no provision save *taqwā*, and no work save patience.'

Abū Saʿīd al-Kharrāz[06] said, 'Anyone who thinks that through his effort

---

01 Sarī al-Saqaṭī (d. 251 AH). Renowned Sufi saint of Baghdad who was the uncle and spiritual master of Imām al-Junayd.

02 Imām Abu'l Qāsim al-Junayd (d. 298 AH). Most famous link in the major Sufi chain. Most Sufi orders in existence today trace their chains back to him. He lived and taught in Baghdad and was also a jurist of the *madhhab* of Abū Thawr.

03 Al-Ḥārith al-Muḥāsibī (d. 247 AH). Great early Sufi, Scholar, and spiritual writer of Baghdad who influenced Imām al-Ghazālī.

04 Yaḥyā ibn Muʿādh al-Rāzī (d. 258 AH). Sufi sage of Nishapur whose utterances are often quoted on works of Sufism.

05 Sahl ibn ʿAbdallāh al-Tustarī (d. 283 AH) Renowned Persian Sufi from Tustar

06 Abū Saʿīd al-Kharrāz (d. 277 or 286 AH). A great Sufi of Baghdad. He kept company

he will arrive is tiring himself, and anyone who thinks that without effort he will arrive is indulging in wishful thinking.'

'Abdal-Wahhāb al-Shaʿrānī[01] said, 'I once saw Manṣūr ibn ʿAmmār[02] in a dream and asked him what God had done with him and he replied, "He made me stand before Him and said, 'You are Manṣūr ibn ʿAmmār?' I said, 'Yes O Lord!' 'Are you the one who strove to make people renounce the world while desiring it himself?' 'That was so, but I never once sat in company without beginning by praising You, then invoking blessings on Your Prophet Muḥammad—may blessings and peace be on him—then giving counsels to your servants.' so He said—August and Majestic is He—, 'He has spoken the truth! Erect a chair for him that he may glorify Me in My Heaven among My Angels as he has glorified Me in My earth among My servants'."'

It has been related that a young slave once passed by Manṣūr ibn ʿAmmār and heard him say, 'I shall make four prayers for the one who will give this poor man four dirhams.' The boy had four dirhams which his master, a merchant, had given him to buy things. He gave them to the poor man and obtained his four prayers, and returned empty-handed to his master, who asked him what the four prayers were. He said, 'That God the Exalted should free me from slavery.' So the man set him free. He continued, 'That God should compensate me.' His master answered, 'I will give your four thousand dirhams. What about the third one?' He replied, 'That God should grant me and you repentance.' 'I repent to God!' cried the merchant. 'What about the fourth?' 'That God should forgive me, you, the one who reminded us, and everyone else.' He said, 'As for this one it is not in my power.' That same night the man beheld in his sleep the Real—Who is High and Majestic—and He said to him, 'Will I fail to do what is Mine when you have done what is yours? I forgive you, the boy, the one who reminded you, and everyone else!'

Transcendent is God the Exalted! How Generous, Magnanimous, Great,

---

with many masters among who were Dhu'l-Nūn al-Miṣrī and Bishr al-Ḥāfī.

01 'Abdal-Wahhāb al-Shaʿrānī (d. 973 AH). Great Azhari scholar, jurist, and Sufi. He authored a great number of books among the most important of which is *al-Mīzān al-Kubrā* (The Great Balance) on juristic differences between schools. His numerous other works are still widely circulated today.

02 Manṣūr ibn ʿAmmār (d. around 200 AH) Great Sufi who hailed from Khurasan and lived and died in Iraq. His sayings are quoted by Imam Qushayrī in his *Risāla*.

and Compassionate is He! The Benefactor, there is no God save Him; to Him is the Final End.

Let this be the last of what God the Exalted has rendered easy for us to record in this book. God is the Guide to what is true and appropriate, and unto Him is the Return. May God bless and grant peace to His slave and Messenger ﷺ, to whom He entrusted His Revelation, our patron and master Muḥammad ﷺ, who was sent as a Mercy to the Worlds and a Seal to the Prophets, and to his pure and fragrant offspring, his rightly-guided and rightly-guiding Companions, and those who follow them with excellence until Judgment. Praise belongs to God, Lord of the Worlds.

> **Say: This is my way, I summon to God clear sightedly, I and those who follow me, Exalted is God! And I am not of the idolaters.**[116]

Dictation ended on the morning of Thursday, the twelfth of Safar of the year 1130 of the Emigration of the Prophet ﷺ.

We had stopped dictating these chapters some time ago for no obvious reason other than our wish to add to them others that had affinity and harmony with them. A long time elapsed and they remained incomplete. However, some people copied them, and so we became determined to complete them by the grace of God, beginning with the chapter on Rectitude. The latter chapters are not entirely complementary to the earlier ones, but they contain important benefits derived from good sources for those who reflect with fairness and good judgment. We are, as ever, cognizant of the favor of God, the blessings of the Messenger of God ﷺ and the blessings of our Righteous Predecessors to whom we claim attachment and whose way we wish to follow and emulate. May God grant us this, as well as to our parents, children, loved ones, companions, and all Muslims, and may He grant us a good conclusion to our lives accompanied with wellbeing, protection, and safety from all outward and inward temptations.

It is as God wishes; there is no power save by God.[117] He is Sufficient for us and a good Patron. **Your forgiveness, O Lord! To You is the Becoming.**[118]

Endnotes

1. Qur'ān, 2:32.
2. Qur'ān, 67:14.
3. Qur'ān, 57:2, 3.
4. Qur'ān, 2:254.
5. Qur'ān, 35:2.
6. Qur'ān, 2:269.
7. Qur'ān, 11:88.
8. Qur'ān, 7:146.
9. Qur'ān, 40:35.
10. Qur'ān, 53:29.
11. Qur'ān, 18:28.
12. Bayhaqī, *Shuʿab al-īmān*, 6188; Ṭabarānī, *Duʿā*, 1048.
13. Ibn Māja, *Sunan*, 1690; Nasā'ī, *al-Sunan al-Kubrā*, 3236.
14. Muslim, *Ṣaḥīḥ*, 1955.
15. Ṭabarānī, *Kabīr*, 6942; Al-Shihāb al-Quḍāʿī', *Musnad*, 148.
16. Tirmidhī, *Sunan*, 2670.
17. Muslim, *Ṣaḥīḥ*, 2674.
18. Bukhārī, *Ṣaḥīḥ*, 6622.
19. The *Ḥadīth Qudsī* up until here is to be found in: Bayhaqī, *Kitāb al-Iʿtiqād*, 1:145; Al-Muttaqī al-Hindī, *Kanz al-ʿUmmāl*, 587.
20. Tirmidhī, *Sunan*, 2320; Ibn Māja, *Sunan*, 4110.
21. Bayhaqī, *al-Sunan al-Kubrā*, 6102; *Shuʿab al-īmān*, 5819.
22. Ṭabarānī, *Awsaṭ*, 1917.
23. Qur'ān, 17:29.
24. Qur'ān, 25:67.
25. Qur'ān, 3:159.
26. Qur'ān, 7:199.
27. Qur'ān, 25:63.
28. Bukhārī, *Ṣaḥīḥ*, 6927.
29. Muslim, *Ṣaḥīḥ*, 2594.
30. Bukhārī, *Ṣaḥīḥ*, 3560.
31. Aḥmad, *Musnad*, 20512; Bayhaqī, *Shuʿab al-Īmān*, 5032.
32. Qur'ān, 41:35.
33. Aḥmad, *Musnad*, 20512; Bayhaqī, *Ādāb*, 308.
34. Al-Ḥāfiẓ al-ʿIrāqī, when referencing the *ḥadīths* of the *Iḥyā*, said that he found no reference for it and Imām Shawkānī declared it spurious.
35. Al-Ḥākim, *Mustadrak*, 6535; Ṭabarānī, *Kabīr*, 424.
36. Qur'ān, 33:30.
37. Qur'ān, 42:23.
38. Qur'ān, 24:20.
39. Bukhārī, *Ṣaḥīḥ*, 6488.
40. Ibn Māja, *Sunan*, 221; Ibn Ḥibbān, *Ṣaḥīḥ*, 3310.
41. Tirmidhī, *Sunan*, 1987.
42. Ibn Abī Shayba, *Muṣannaf*, 34325; Ṭabarānī, *Kabīr*, 331, 374.

43. No reference was found for this *ḥadīth*.
44. Abū Dāwūd, *Sunan*, 4833.
45. Bukhārī, *Ṣaḥīḥ*, 5534.
46. Bayhaqī, *Shuʿab al-Īmān*, 4639; Al-Ḥākim, *Mustadrak*, 5466.
47. Bukhārī, *Ṣaḥīḥ*, 6168.
48. Abū Dāwūd, *Sunan*, 4031.
49. Muslim, *Ṣaḥīḥ*, 1599.
50. Tirmidhī, *Sunan*, 2451.
51. Tirmidhī, *Sunan*, 2518.
52. Qur'ān, 29:6.
53. Qur'ān, 41:35, 36.
54. Qur'ān, 46:13–4.
55. Ibn Māja, *Sunan*, 277, 278.
56. Nasā'ī, *al-Sunan al-Kubrā*, 11812; Ibn Ḥibbān, *Ṣaḥīḥ*, 942.
57. Nasā'ī, *al-Sunan al-Kubrā*, 11776; Ibn Ḥibbān, *Ṣaḥīḥ*, 350, 660.
58. Qur'ān, 28:83.
59. Qur'ān, 42:20.
60. Tirmidhī, *Sunan*, 2459.
61. Tirmidhī, *Sunan*, 2333.
62. Qur'ān, 39:22.
63. Al-Ḥākim, *Mustadrak*, 7863; Bayhaqī, *Shuʿab al-Īmān*, 10068.
64. Qur'ān, 7:179.
65. Ibn Ḥibbān, *Ṣaḥīḥ*, 6352; Aḥmad, *Musnad*, 2744–3709.
66. Tirmidhī, *Sunan*, 2320.
67. Muslim, *Ṣaḥīḥ*, 2956.
68. Qur'ān, 29:6.
69. Qur'ān, 41:35.
70. Qur'ān, 33:38.
71. Qur'ān, 2:137.
72. Bukhārī, *Ṣaḥīḥ*, 2651, 2652, 3650.
73. Nuʿaym ibn Ḥammād, *Kitāb al-Fitan*, 1614; al-Ḥākim, *Mustadrak*, 4351.
74. Qur'ān, 2:281.
75. Qur'ān, 3:200.
76. Qur'ān, 4:59
77. Qur'ān, 5:93.
78. Qur'ān, 7:199.
79. Qur'ān, 10:61.
80. Qur'ān, 11:15.
81. Qur'ān, 12:53.
82. Qur'ān, 15:88.
83. Qur'ān, 16:128.
84. Qur'ān, 18:110.
85. Qur'ān, 20:132.
86. Qur'ān, 23:115.
87. Qur'ān, 29:69.
88. Qur'ān, 33:72.
89. Qur'ān, 39:67.
90. Qur'ān, 45:21.
91. Qur'ān, 59:18.
92. Qur'ān, 28:8.
93. Ibn Māja, *Sunan*, 1081.
94. Muslim, *Ṣaḥīḥ*, 118.
95. Tirmidhī, *Sunan*, 2450.
96. Bayhaqī, *Shuʿab al-Īmān*, 730.
97. Tirmidhī, *Sunan*, 2317.
98. Tirmidhī, *Sunan*, 2518.
99. Bukhārī, *Ṣaḥīḥ*, 13.
100. Abū Dāwūd, *Sunan*, 4797.
101. Ṭabarānī, *Awsaṭ*, 8938; Dāraquṭnī, *Sunan*, 4396, 4814.
102. Muslim, *Ṣaḥīḥ*, 49.
103. Ibn Abī ʿĀṣim, *al-Sunna*, 15; Al-Ḥakīm al-Tirmidhī, *Nawādir al-Uṣūl*, 4:164.
104. Muslim, *Ṣaḥīḥ*, 35.
105. Tirmidhī, *Sunan*, 2601
106. Muslim, *Ṣaḥīḥ*, 2822.
107. Tirmidhī, *Sunan*, 2380.
108. Daylamī, *al-Firdaws*, 338–339. The hadith runs as follows:

Wear wool and eat half your stomach fill, for this is one part of Prophethood.

109. Bayhaqī, *Shu'ab al-Īmān*, 6865.
110. Bukhārī, *Ṣaḥīḥ*, 660.
111. Bazzār, *Musnad*, 6237; Bayhaqī, *Shu'ab al-Īmān*, 10079.
112. 'Abdal-Ḥaqq ibn 'Abdal-Raḥmān al-Ishbīlī, *Al-'Āqiba fi dhikr al-mawt*, 1:39.
113. Tirmidhī, *Sunan*, 2417.
114. Qur'ān, 59:10.
115. Qur'ān, 16:90.
116. Qur'ān, 12:108.
117. Qur'ān, 18:39
118. Qur'ān, 2:285

Imām ʿAbdallāh ibn ʿAlawī al-Ḥaddād

Imām ʿAbdallāh ibn ʿAlawī al-Ḥaddād was born in his parents' summer cottage on the outskirts of the town of Tarīm in the Ḥaḍramawt Valley in 1044 AH in the 3rd decade of the eighteenth century CE.

He grew up in Tarīm, losing his sight when he was around four. As a child he liked to play, and with enthusiasm, like other children, but was also keen to pray, fast, recite the Quran and study the religious sciences. He was a frequent visitor to the graves of his ancestors in the cemetery of Tarīm. As he walked the streets of Tarīm with his friends, they read Sufi books and chanted Sufi poems.

As a teenager, he went around the mosques of Tarīm at night, making it a point to pray in every single one of them. He also made it a point to visit every man of God in the area to benefit from both their knowledge and their spirituality. In Ramaḍān of 1061 AH he moved to the small Hujayra mosque, to live in the small rooms on the roof known as the *zāwiya* where he spent the next thirty-eight years, before moving to the south-eastern suburb of al-Ḥāwī. He became an accomplished scholar and major saint at an early age and soon the time came when he was formally ordered, first by his ancestors, then by the Prophet ﷺ to hold teaching sessions.

Despite his blindness, the Imām was a voracious reader, spending a substantial amount of time listening to books being read to him. He was later to say, "We do not think there is a single book in the whole of Ḥaḍramawt that we have not either read, been told about its contents, heard parts of it, or heard about it." This, together with an acute intelligence and remarkable capacity for celar thinking led him eventually to attain the status of independent scholar, drawing his knowledge directly from the Quran and *Sunna*, without recourse to the works of previous scholars.

When the Zaydī Shīʿa of Northern Yemen invaded Ḥaḍramawt, the Imām wrote the litany entitled *al-Rātib* and included in it statements of correct creed to protect the beliefs of the people from the Muʿtazilite deviancy of the conquerors. Later on, when he went to *Ḥajj*, the daily recitation of the *Rātib* was instituted in the Sacred Mosque in Makka and the Prophet's Mosque in Madina.

In 1099 AH, the year his son Ḥasan was born, the Imām moved to al-Ḥāwī, to the house that belonged to his maternal grandfather. There he held teaching sessions every afternoon and some mornings, and had private sessions with *Ḥabīb* Aḥmad ibn Zayn al-Ḥabashī on the landing between the ground and first floors of his house.

During the forty-eight years, he lived there he never stopped teaching, counselling, feeding countless guests, and looking after the poor and the weak. He educated and disciplined many students who became in their turn illustrious leaders. He was acknowledged by the great men of his time, both those who knew him personally and those who had only heard of him, as having reached the supreme degree in sanctity

He saw fit to adapt the Sufi method of his ancestors to the conditions of his time and even more so the times to come, in the belief that it was no longer suitable, for the people had become incapable of accepting the old manner of unconditional surrender entirely to the master and unquestioning obedience, and incapable of performing the taxing spiritual exercises performed by the previous generations of Sufis. Translated into everyday behavior, this meant that the disciple must follow the basic Islamic pattern of avoiding all things forbidden or disapproved by the Sacred Law and carefully performing all that is prescribed as obligatory or recommended. Then he should occupy his time with remembering God by reading the Quran and reciting the various litanies and invocations prescribed by the *Sunna*, for which he should acquire a minimum of necessary religious knowledge. He should then improve his moral character by striving to develop the virtues of compassion, forgiveness, tolerance, patience, and generosity, all of which require an arduous struggle against the ego. This pattern the Imām called the "Path of the Companions of the Right Hand" to differentiate it from the "Path of the Drawn Near", which was the more arduous path of their ancestors. He liked discretion as regards the inward realities of the Path and was very careful never to cause confusion or sedition, or induce people to think ill of any man of God.

He authored nine books of greatly variable lengths all of which have been translated, among other languages, into English and published under the following titles: *Counsels of religion*, *The Complete Summons and General Reminder*, *The Book of Assistance*, *Mutual Reminding*, *The Lives of man*, *Gifts for the Seeker*, *Knowledge and Wisdom*, *Good Manners of the Spiritual Disciple*, and *The Aphorisms*. Answers to questions gleaned from his correspondence and compiled by *Ḥabīb* Aḥmad ibn Zayn al-Ḥabashī formed another volume the English translation of which was published as *The Sublime Treasures*. He also left a voluminous collection of poems collected in his *Diwān*, an even more voluminous correspondence, and his utterances recorded by one of his disciples and collected in a five volumes manuscript.

Imām al-Ḥaddād died in his house of al-Ḥāwī on Tuesday the 7th of Dhul-Qaʿda of the year 1132 AH. and was buried at the Cemetery of Zanbal.

Dr. Mostafa al-Badawi

Dr. Mostafa al-Badawi is a Consultant Psychiatrist and a member of the Royal College of Psychiatrists. He was classically trained in the Islamic sciences and studied under many traditional scholars, foremost among whom is the late Habib Ahmad Mashur al-Haddad (may God have mercy upon him and shower him with light in his grave). Dr. Badawi is also one of the leading contemporary translators of classical Islamic books from Arabic into English as well as an accomplished author. His translations include: *The Book of Assistance*, *The Lives of Man*, *Key to the Garden*, *Degrees of the Soul*, *Knowledge and Wisdom*, *Gifts for the Seeker*, *Mutual Reminding and Good Manners of the Disciple*, *The Sublime Treasures*, *Counsels of Religion*, *the Prophetic Invocations*, *The Aphorisms and Sufi Sage of Arabia*. His own works include: *Man and the Universe*, *A Blessed Valley*, *Ancient Prophets of Arabia*, *A Higher Reality: Manifestations of the Unseen and Twilight of a World.*